GCSE Physics for CCEA

second edition

Frank McCauley
Roy White

Endorsed by CCEA on 17th July 2011. If in any doubt about the continuing currency of CCEA endorsement, please contact Heather Clarke at CCEA, 29 Clarendon Road, Belfast, BT1 3BG.

Acknowledgements

The Publisher would like to thank the following for permission to reproduce copyright material:

Photo credits
p.19 © Stanislaw Kujawa/Alamy; **p.22** © Imagestate Media; **p.25** *l* © Worldspec/NASA/Alamy, *m* © Tom Hirtreiter – Fotolia, *r* © Science Photo Library; **p.26** *t* © Science Photo Library, *b* © Artur Shevel – Fotolia.com; **p.32** © Gary Hawkins/Rex Features; **p.45** *l* © Steve Cukrov – Fotolia, *r* © Keystone USA-ZUMA/Rex Features; **p.63** *t* © Medical-on-Line/Alamy, *b* © Medical-on-Line/Alamy; **p.64** © Chris Priest/Science Photo Library; **p.83** © Darren Brode – Fotolia; **p.89** *t* © microimages – Fotolia, *b* © sciencephotos/Alamy; **p.102** © Imagestate Media; **p.103** *t* © Steven May/Alamy, *b* © imagebroker/Alamy; **p.111** *t* © Ria Novosti/Science Photo Library, *m* © Lester Lefkowitz/Stone/Getty Images, *b* © yuri4u80 – Fotolia; **p.112** © Chris Knapton/Science Photo Library; **p.114** © sciencephotos/Alamy; **p.121** *t* © Andrew Lambert Photography/Science Photo Library, *tm* © Andrew Lambert Photography/Science Photo Library, *m* © Martyn F. Chillmaid/Science Photo Library, *bm* © Andrew Lambert Photography/Science Photo Library, *b* © sciencephotos/Alamy; **p.132** *tl* © Panasonic UK, *tr* Konstantin Gushcha – Fotolia, *bl* © misterryba – Fotolia, *bm* Jaroslaw Grudzinski – Fotolia, *br* Jamie Kingham/Getty Images; **p.135** *both* © Andrew Lambert Photography/Science Photo Library; **p.145** © Design Pics Inc/Rex Features; **p.148** © Andrew Lambert Photography/Science Photo Library; **p.150** Sipa Press/Rex Features; **p.154** © JoeFox/Alamy.

t = top, *b* = bottom, *l* = left, *r* = right, *m* = middle

Every effort has been made to trace all copyright holders, but if any have been inadvertently overlooked, the Publisher will be pleased to make the necessary arrangements at the first opportunity.

Although every effort has been made to ensure that website addresses are correct at time of going to press, Hodder Education cannot be held responsible for the content of any website mentioned. It is sometimes possible to find a relocated web page by typing in the address of the home page for a website in the URL window of your browser.

Orders: please contact Bookpoint Ltd, 130 Milton Park, Abingdon, Oxon OX14 4SB. Telephone: (44) 01235 827720. Fax: (44) 01235 400454. Lines are open 9.00–17.00, Monday to Saturday, with a 24-hour message answering service. Visit our website at www.hoddereducation.co.uk

© 2011 Frank McCauley and Roy White

First published in 2011 by
Hodder Education
An Hachette UK Company,
338 Euston Road
London NW1 3BH

Impression number	5	4	3	2	1
Year	2015	2014	2013	2012	2011

All rights reserved. Apart from any use permitted under UK copyright law, no part of this publication may be reproduced or transmitted in any form or by any means, electronic or mechanical, including photocopying and recording, or held within any information storage and retrieval system, without permission in writing from the publisher or under licence from the Copyright Licensing Agency Limited. Further details of such licences (for reprographic reproduction) may be obtained from the Copyright Licensing Agency Limited, Saffron House, 6–10 Kirby Street, London EC1N 8TS.

Cover photo © Dick Luria/Science Photo Library

Illustrations by Barking Dog Art

Typeset in 12/14 Bembo by Tech-Set Limited

A catalogue record for this title is available from the British Library

ISBN 978 0340 983812

Contents

Chapter 1	**Motion**	1
Chapter 2	**Forces**	13
Chapter 3	**Energy**	36
Chapter 4	**Radioactivity**	58
Chapter 5	**Waves, sound and light**	74
Chapter 6	**Electricity**	108
Chapter 7	**Electromagnetism**	143
Chapter 8	**The Earth and Universe**	160
Controlled Assessment Task		177
Index		179

Preface

The GCSE Science for CCEA series comprises three books: GCSE Biology for CCEA, GCSE Chemistry for CCEA and GCSE Physics for CCEA, which together cover all aspects of the material needed for students following the CCEA GCSE specifications in:

* Science: Double Award
* Science: Biology
* Science: Chemistry
* Science: Physics

GCSE Physics for CCEA covers all the material relating to the physics component of the CCEA Science Double Award, together with the additional material required for the CCEA Science: Physics specification.

Frank McCauley and Roy White are both physics teachers and examiners.

Identifying Specification and Tier

The material required for each specification and tier is clearly identified using the following colour code:

All material not on a tinted background is required for foundation tier students following either the GCSE Double Award Science or the GCSE Physics specifications.

Material required for the higher tier students following either the GCSE Double Award Science or the GCSE Physics specification is identified with a green tinted background.

Material required for foundation tier students following the GCSE Physics specification is identified with a blue tinted background.

Material required for higher tier students following the GCSE Physics specification is identified with a red tinted background.

Controlled Assessment of Practical Skills

During your course you will be required to carry out a number of controlled assessment tasks.

Double Award Science students complete **two** controlled assessment tasks from a choice of six supplied by CCEA at the start of the course. The two tasks must come from different subject areas within the specification. So, for example, they cannot both come from the physics section of the Double Award Science specification.

For GCSE Physics students, CCEA sets two comparable tasks at the start of the course. Candidates must take at least **one** of these controlled assessment tasks in the course of the two years.

For both GCSE Double Award Science and GCSE Physics, a student cannot take a specific task more than once.

Further details about the nature of the Controlled Assessment Task (the CAT) is given within this book.

1 Motion

▶ Motion in a straight line

Distance and displacement

The **distance** between Belfast and Coleraine is 100 km.

But the **displacement** of Belfast from Coleraine is 100 km south-east. We can define displacement as *distance in a specified direction*. Displacement is represented by an arrow – the length of the arrow is proportional to the distance, and the direction of the arrow is in the same direction as the displacement (Figure 2).

Figure 1 The distance between Coleraine and Belfast

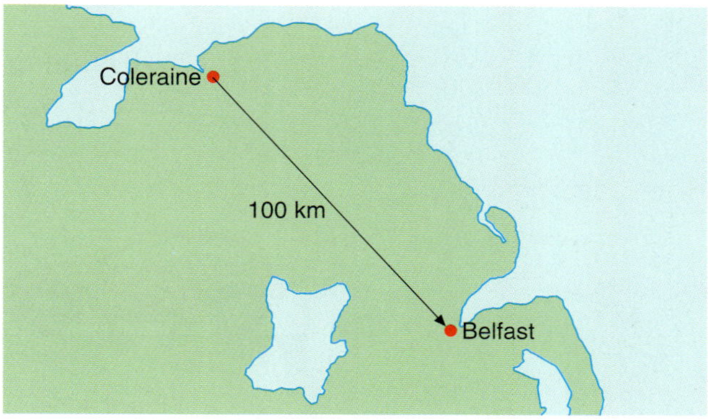

Figure 2 The displacement of Belfast from Coleraine

The return journey from Coleraine to Belfast and then back again is a distance of 200 km, but the displacement is 0 km!

We say that distance is a **scalar quantity** – a quantity with size only – whereas displacement is a **vector quantity** because it has size *and* direction.

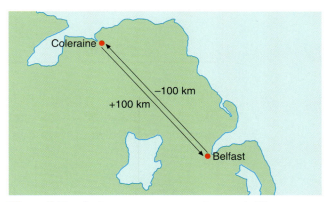

Figure 3 The displacement on a return journey is 0 km

Speed

If a car travels between two points on a road, its average speed can be calculated using the formula:

$$\text{speed} = \frac{\text{distance moved}}{\text{time taken}}$$

MOTION

If distance is measured in metres (m) and time in seconds (s), speed is measured in metres per second (m/s).

For example, if a car travels from Coleraine to Belfast in 2 hours, its average speed is:

$$\frac{100}{2} = 50\,\text{km/h}$$

The speedometer would certainly not read 50 km/h for the whole journey and would vary considerably from this value. The driver may decide to stop for a rest or might overtake another car and be travelling faster than 50 km/h. Hence we talk about the **average speed**, the formula for which is:

$$\text{average speed} = \frac{\text{total distance moved}}{\text{time taken}}$$

To find the actual speed at a particular moment in time, we would need to know the distance travelled in a very short interval of time.

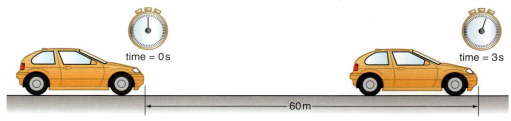

Figure 4 Measuring speed

> **DID YOU KNOW?**
> The fastest passenger airliner is the Russian Tupolev Tu-144. It is reported to have reached a maximum speed of 1600 miles/hour – or Mach 2.4.

Example
Find the speed of a car that travels 60 m in 3 s.

Answer

$$\text{speed} = \frac{\text{distance}}{\text{time}}$$

$$= \frac{60}{3}$$

$$= \mathbf{20\,m/s}$$

Velocity

Whereas speed is the distance travelled in unit time, **velocity** is the distance travelled in unit time in a specified direction.

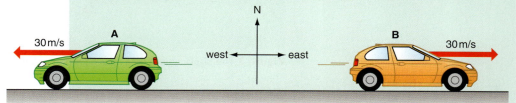

Figure 5 These two cars have the same speed – but different velocities

Looking at Figure 5, car A has the same speed as car B but a different velocity. Car A's velocity is 30 m/s due west, while car B has a velocity of 30 m/s due east.

Speed is a scalar quantity and velocity is a vector quantity.

Because displacement is the distance travelled in a specified direction, we can rewrite the formula for velocity as:

$$\text{velocity} = \frac{\text{displacement}}{\text{time taken}}$$

The units for speed and velocity are the same, metres per second (m/s). Occasionally, you will see the units of kilometres per hour (km/h).

The car in Figure 6 is moving at a steady, or constant, speed of 20 m/s along a straight road and then goes around a bend.

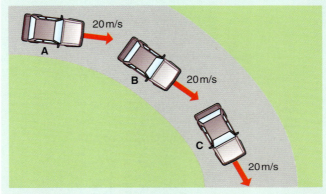

Figure 6 The velocity of the car changes as it goes around the bend

The speed of the car at A, B and C is 20 m/s, but the velocity changes as it travels from A to B to C. This is because velocity is a vector quantity and although the size of the velocity may be constant at 20 m/s, its direction is constantly changing, so its velocity is constantly changing.

Acceleration

When the velocity of a body increases or decreases, we say it accelerates. Consider the example in Figure 7.

Figure 7 This car is accelerating

The car starts from rest (velocity = 0 m/s), but after 1 second its velocity has increased to 3 m/s. After 2 seconds its velocity has increased by 3 m/s to 6 m/s. We say that the car's velocity increases by 3 m/s in 1 second due east – i.e. its **acceleration** is 3 m/s² due east.

We can define acceleration as the change in velocity in unit time:

$$\text{acceleration} = \frac{\text{change in velocity}}{\text{time taken}}$$

Acceleration is measured in metres per second per second, written as m/s². Because acceleration is a vector quantity, it can be shown using an arrow (often double-headed). Alternatively, a '+' or '−' sign can be used to indicate whether the velocity is increasing or decreasing. For example:

$+3 \text{ m/s}^2$ (velocity increasing by 3 m/s every second)

-3 m/s^2 (velocity decreasing by 3 m/s every second)

A negative acceleration is called a **deceleration** or a **retardation**. A uniform acceleration means a constant (steady) acceleration. In terms of symbols:

if v = final velocity

u = initial velocity

t = time taken,

then $v - u$ = change in velocity

and acceleration, $a = \dfrac{v - u}{t}$

Multiplying across by t

$at = v - u$

or $v = u + at$

Questions

1. A car travels 800 m in 40 s.
   a) What is its average speed?
   b) Why is its actual speed probably different from its average speed?
2. A car has a steady speed of 10 m/s.
   a) How far does the car travel in 9 s?
   b) How long does it take the car to travel 220 m?
3. Explain the difference between:
   a) distance and displacement   b) speed and velocity.
4. Calculate the average speed of each of these objects:

   a) This runner travels 400 m in 44 s.
   b) This car travels 175 miles in 3 hours.
   c) This shuttle travels 43 750 km in 2.5 hours.
5. a) A train has an acceleration of 3 m/s². What does this tell you about the velocity of the train?
   b) A bus has a deceleration of 2 m/s². What does this tell you about the velocity of the bus?
6. A car takes 8 s to increase its velocity from 3 m/s to 30 m/s. What is its acceleration?

GRAPHS AND MOTION

7 A motorbike, travelling at 25 m/s, takes 5 s to come to a halt. What is its deceleration?

8 An aircraft has a uniform acceleration of 4 m/s² on take-off.
  a) What velocity does the aircraft gain in 5 s?
  b) If the aircraft passes a point on the runway at a velocity of 28 m/s, what will its velocity be 8 s later?

9 A ball is thrown vertically upwards in the air, leaving the hand at 30 m/s. The acceleration due to gravity is 10 m/s².

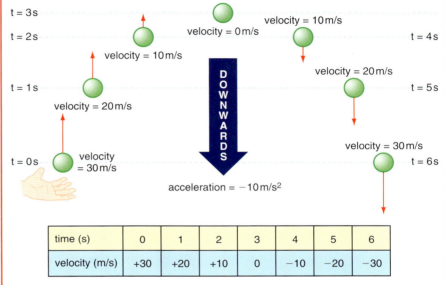

time (s)	0	1	2	3	4	5	6
velocity (m/s)	+30	+20	+10	0	−10	−20	−30

Draw a graph to show the motion of the ball. Plot velocity on the y-axis and time on the x-axis.

▶ Graphs and motion

Graphs are a very useful way of displaying the motion of objects. There are two main types of graphs used in physics:

* distance–time graph
* velocity–time graph.

Distance–time graphs

A **distance–time graph** is a plot of distance on the y-axis versus time on the x-axis.

The simplest type of distance–time graph is shown in Figure 8.

This graph illustrates that although the time increases steadily, the distance travelled is not changing. The body must be **stationary**.

A horizontal line on a distance–time graph means that the body is stationary.

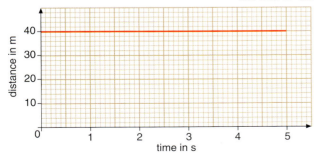

Figure 8 A simple distance–time graph of a stationary body

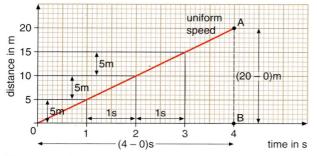

Figure 9 A distance–time graph of a body moving with uniform speed

In contrast, Figure 9 shows that the distance is increasing by 5 m in every second – i.e. the body is travelling with uniform speed, covering equal distances in equal units of time. The slope or gradient of a distance–time graph represents the speed. The speed the body in Figure 9 is travelling is 5 m/s.

$$\text{The slope of the graph} = \frac{AB}{OB}$$
$$= \frac{20 - 0}{4 - 0}$$
$$= \mathbf{5\ m/s}$$

When the velocity is changing, the slope of the distance–time graph changes. In Figure 10, the slope is increasing, which means that the body is accelerating.

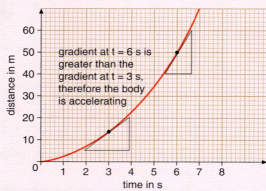

Figure 10 A distance–time graph for a body that is accelerating

Velocity–time graphs

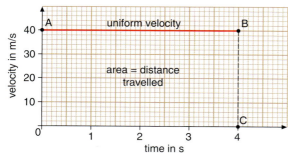

Figure 11 A velocity–time graph for a car at constant velocity

A **velocity–time graph** is a plot of velocity on the y-axis versus time on the x-axis.

The simplest type of velocity–time graph is shown in Figure 11.

This graph shows that while time is increasing, the velocity remains at a constant (steady) 30 m/s. The car is not accelerating.

The area under a velocity–time graph represents the displacement travelled.

For example, in Figure 11:

$$\text{area of rectangle OABC} = OA \times OC$$
$$= 40 \times 4$$
$$= \mathbf{160\ m}$$

The displacement travelled by the car is 160 m.

In Figure 12, OD is the velocity–time graph for a body accelerating uniformly from rest.

The slope, or gradient, of a velocity–time graph represents the acceleration of the body.

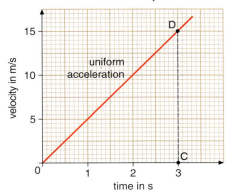

Figure 12 A velocity–time graph for a body accelerating uniformly

In Figure 12:
$$\text{acceleration} = \frac{DC}{OC}$$
$$= \frac{15 - 0}{3 - 0}$$
$$= \frac{15}{3}$$
$$= 5 \text{ m/s}^2$$

Furthermore, the area of the triangle OCD gives the displacement travelled:
$$\text{displacement} = \text{area of triangle OCD}$$
$$= \tfrac{1}{2} \times OC \times CD$$
$$= \tfrac{1}{2} \times 3 \times 15$$
$$= 22.5 \text{ m}$$

The relationship between average velocity, time and displacement

Consider a general graph, Figure 13, of a body uniformly accelerated from an initial velocity u to a final velocity v under an acceleration a for a time of t seconds.

The area of the trapezium is the displacement s.

s = average of the parallel sides $\times$ base

$$s = \tfrac{1}{2}(u + v)t$$

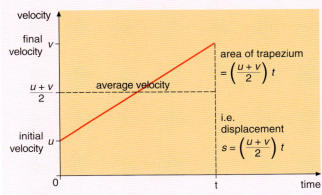

Figure 13 Graph showing the relationship between velocity, time and displacement

Questions

10 Paul and Jim set off at the same time from their separate houses to walk to a nearby shop.

The table below shows the distances travelled by Paul to the shop.

Distance walked by Paul in m	0	3	6	9	12	15	18	21
Time elapsed in seconds	0	1	2	3	4	5	6	7

a) Draw a graph of distance against time for Paul's journey.

The table below shows the distances travelled by Jim to the same shop.

Distance walked by Jim in m	0	2	4	6	8	10	12	14
Time elapsed in seconds	0	1	2	3	4	5	6	7

b) Draw a graph of distance against time for Jim's journey on the same axis.

c) Use the graphs to answer the following questions.
  i) Which walker is going faster?
  ii) How long does it take Paul and Jim to walk 11 m?
  iii) How far apart are Paul and Jim after 2.5 s?
  iv) Is Paul's speed steady?
  v) What is Jim's average speed?

11 Study the velocity–time graph below and describe in words the motion of the object.

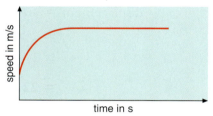

12 The diagram below shows a velocity–time graph for a car accelerating away from a junction. Calculate:
  a) the acceleration during the first 5 s
  b) the total displacement.

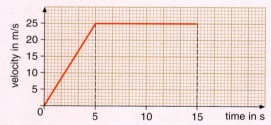

13 The graph below represents a journey in a lift in a hospital.

a) Briefly describe the motion represented by i) OA ii) AB iii) BC.
b) Use the graph to calculate:
   i)   the initial acceleration of the lift
   ii) the total distance travelled by the lift
   iii) the average speed of the lift for the whole journey.

Use a graphical method or formulae to answer questions 14–20.

14 A car accelerates at 3 m/s² for 10 seconds. If it started with a velocity of 20 m/s, calculate its final velocity.

15 An ice-skater moves off from rest (this means that $u = 0$ m/s) with a uniform acceleration of 0.3 m/s². What is her speed and distance travelled after 10 s?

16 A stone is thrown vertically upwards with a velocity of 20 m/s. Find how high it will go and the time taken to reach this height (assume $g = 10$ m/s²). Ignore air resistance.
  (**Hint:** g is acting in the opposite direction to the velocity so it must be given a negative sign.)

17 A stone is dropped down an empty mine shaft, taking 3 seconds to reach the bottom. Assuming that the stone falls from rest and accelerates at 10 m/s², calculate:
  a) the maximum speed reached by the stone before hitting the bottom
  b) the average speed of the stone in flight
  c) the depth of the mine shaft.

18 A helicopter at a height of 500 m drops a package, which falls to the ground without its parachute opening. Neglecting air resistance and assuming that the acceleration is constant and equal to 10 m/s², calculate:
  a) the time taken for the package to reach the ground
  b) the velocity with which it hits the ground.

19 A ball is thrown vertically upwards into the air with a velocity of 50 m/s. Neglecting air resistance and assuming that the acceleration is constant and equal to 10 m/s², calculate:
  a) the time taken to reach maximum height
  b) the maximum height reached by the ball.

20 A cyclist accelerates at 3 m/s².
  a) What is his speed after 5 s?
  He then decelerates at 0.5 m/s².
  b) How long will it take for his speed to reach zero, and how far will he have travelled?
  c) Draw a velocity–time graph for this motion.

▶ Friction and motion

A car engine produces the forwards force necessary to keep the car moving. If the car is not accelerating, but is moving at a steady speed, the forwards force from the engine must be balanced by an equal backwards force. This force, called **air resistance** or **drag**, is a force of **friction**.

MOTION

Figure 14 For this car, the forwards force is the engine and the backwards force is friction

In many instances, it is important to maximise the amount of friction between two surfaces in order to increase the amount of grip available. Car brakes and tyres are designed with this in mind. Pushing the brake pedal causes friction between the brake pads and the wheels. This friction slows the wheels and stops the car.

The total stopping distance of a car is made up of two parts:

* the thinking distance
* the braking distance.

The **thinking distance** is how far the car travels in the time that the driver reacts to an emergency and applies the brakes. The **braking distance** is how far the car travels once the brakes have been applied. The larger the braking force, the shorter the braking distance.

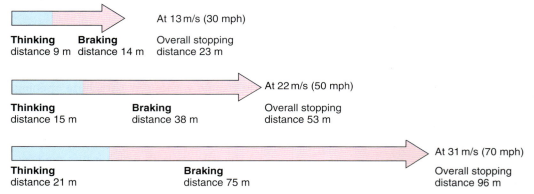

Figure 15 Stopping distances

In icy or wet conditions, the friction between the car tyres and the road is reduced, which reduces the grip and thus increases the braking distance. Under these conditions, a car will not only need a greater stopping distance, but also something to prevent it skidding out of control. The tread pattern on car tyres is designed to remove excess water on the road, providing better grip. The thinking distance can be affected if the driver is tired or distracted or if they have been drinking alcohol or taking drugs.

Speed affects both the thinking distance and the braking distance. The faster a car is travelling, the greater the total stopping distance.

Drag

When an object moves through a fluid (liquid or gas), the opposing frictional forces are usually called **drag**. The amount of drag depends on the shape of the object, and so can be reduced by good design.

EXAM QUESTIONS

▶ Exam questions

1 a) A taxi makes a journey of 3.0 km in 5 minutes. What is its average speed in m/s? Show clearly how you get your answer. *(6 marks)*

b) The velocity–time graph for the return journey is shown below.

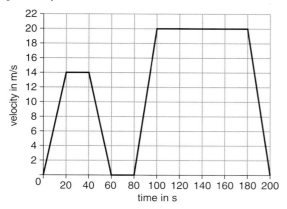

i) What is the acceleration of the taxi during the first 20 seconds? Show clearly how you get your answer. *(5 marks)*

ii) The mass of the taxi and its passengers is 1500 kg. The driving force acting on the taxi for the first 20 s is 3000 N. Calculate the average drag (frictional) force acting on the taxi during this time in newtons. Show clearly how you get your answer. *(7 marks)*

iii) What is the distance travelled from the time of 80 s to the end of the journey? Show clearly how you get your answer. *(6 marks)*

c) Describe the movement of the taxi during the times indicated below.
  i) 20 s to 40 s
  ii) 40 s to 60 s
  iii) 60 s to 80 s *(3 marks)*

d) The mass of the taxi and its passengers is 1500 kg. Calculate the momentum of the taxi and its occupants at a time of 20 s. Show clearly how you get your answer. *(5 marks)*

2 A hovercraft has a mass of 10 000 kg. It hovers at a constant height above the surface of the sea.

a) Calculate the weight of the hovercraft in newtons. *(2 marks)*

b) Write down the size, in newtons, of the upward force exerted by the air cushion below the hovercraft. *(1 mark)*

c) The base of the hovercraft is a rectangle measuring 20 m by 5 m. Use your answer to part **b)** to calculate the upward pressure on the base of the hovercraft in pascals.
Show clearly how you get your answer. *(4 marks)*

The hovercraft now moves to the left at a steady speed, as shown in the diagram below.

d) Copy the diagram and draw an arrow to show the direction of the frictional force on the hovercraft. *(1 mark)*

When the forward force is 15 000 N, the hovercraft moves at a steady speed. The forward force is now increased to 20 000 N, but the size of the frictional force remains unchanged.

e) Calculate the acceleration of the hovercraft when the forward force is 20 000 N. Remember that the mass of the hovercraft is 10 000 kg.
Show clearly how you get your answer. *(4 marks)*

3 Below is a velocity–time graph showing the motion of a train.

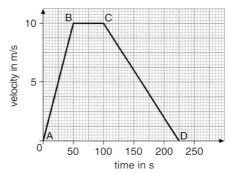

a) How can you tell from the graph that the train is always travelling in the same direction? *(1 mark)*

b) Calculate the acceleration of the train represented by the line AB on the graph. Show clearly how you get your answer. *(3 marks)*

c) At what time does the train driver first apply the brakes? *(1 mark)*

d) Calculate the distance travelled by the train on each of the two stages of the journey, BC and CD. Show clearly how you get your answer.
   i) Distance travelled on stage BC. *(2 marks)*
   ii) Distance travelled on stage CD. *(3 marks)*

e) The distance travelled by the train in the first 50 s of its motion is 250 m. Calculate the average speed of the train during the 225 seconds of its journey. Show clearly how you get your answer. *(3 marks)*

f) During the part of the journey marked BC, the force opposing the motion of the train is 5000 N. Calculate the work done in joules against this force during this part of the journey. Show clearly how you get your answer. *(3 marks)*

4 Recently the Tour de France cycle race started in Dublin. Cyclists A and B started the race at the same time.

a) The graph of distance travelled against time for cyclist A is shown below:

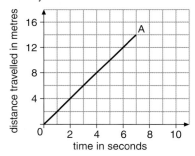

i) What was the speed of cyclist A? Show clearly how you get your answer. *(2 marks)*

ii) For the first 4 seconds, cyclist B had a steady speed of 4 m/s. Copy the grid and draw the graph for cyclist B. Label it B. *(2 marks)*

b) Part of the race took place in the Wicklow Mountains where riders climbed to a height h metres.

i) The total mass of one cyclist and his bike was 80 kg. The gain in potential energy of the cyclist (man and bike) at height h was 320 000 J. Calculate the height h ($g = 10$ m/s^2). Show clearly how you get your answer. *(3 marks)*

ii) Near the finish, the speed of the cyclist was 14 m/s. Calculate the kinetic energy of the cyclist. Show clearly how you get your answer. *(3 marks)*

2 Forces

▶ Balanced and unbalanced forces

A **force** has both size and direction. The size of a force is measured in **newtons** (N). When drawing forces in diagrams, it is usual to represent the direction of the force by an arrow and the size of the force by the length of the arrow drawn to scale.

If two forces are equal in size and opposite in direction, then the forces are balanced. **Balanced** forces do not change the velocity of an object.

Figure 1 shows a car travelling at a steady speed of 30 km/h in a straight line under the action of two equal and opposite forces – the thrust exerted by the engine and drag.

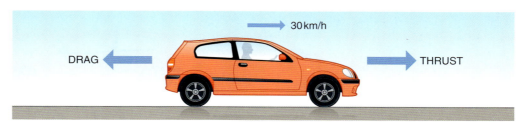

Figure 1

If an object is stationary (not moving), it will remain stationary.

In a tug-of-war (Figure 2), two teams pull against each other. When both teams pull equally hard, the forces are balanced and the rope does not move. But when one team starts to pull with a larger force, the rope moves. When this happens, the two forces are no longer balanced.

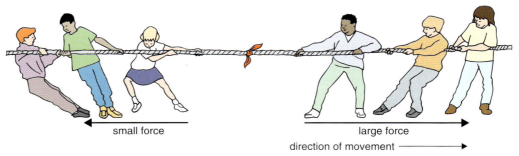

Figure 2 The forces in this tug of war are unbalanced because the team on the right is pulling with a larger force

Unbalanced forces will change the velocity of an object. Since velocity involves both speed and direction, unbalanced forces can make an object speed up, slow down or change direction.

Unbalanced forces applied to the handlebars will make the cyclist in Figure 3 change direction. This means the velocity of the cyclist will change even though the speed may stay the same.

Figure 3

An object will only accelerate when an unbalanced force acts on it. It then accelerates in the direction of the unbalanced force. If the driving force on a car is bigger than the drag force, the car will accelerate or speed up.

Figure 4 This car is accelerating

If the driver then decides to apply the brakes, the driving force will be smaller than the braking force, and the car will decelerate or slow down.

Figure 5 This car is decelerating

A car is travelling in a straight line along a motorway. Table 1 shows in which situations there is an unbalanced force on the car.

Situation	Unbalanced force acting
The car's speed is increasing	✓
The car's speed is decreasing	✓
The car's speed is constant	
The car starts going round a bend	✓

Table 1

⇨ DID YOU KNOW?

There are four fundamental forces in the Universe that account for all interactions between matter and energy. They are known as the *strong nuclear*, *weak nuclear*, *electromagnetic* and *gravitational* forces. The most powerful of these is the strong nuclear force which is 100 times stronger than the next strongest, the electromagnetic force.

▶ Newton's laws

All that we have said about forces so far is summarised by **Newton's first law**:

> A body stays at rest or continues to move in a straight line with constant speed (uniform velocity), unless an unbalanced force makes it behave differently.

Linking unbalanced forces, mass and acceleration

It is possible for one person to push a car – but the acceleration of the car would be small. The more people pushing the car, the larger the acceleration. So, the larger the force, the larger the acceleration.

NEWTON'S LAWS

Figure 6

Even four people would find it difficult to push a van, because the mass of a van is far larger than the mass of a car. The larger the mass, the smaller the acceleration.

Figure 7

The size of the force needed to accelerate a mass can be worked out using **Newton's second law**:

$$\begin{aligned} \text{unbalanced force} &= \text{mass} \times \text{acceleration} \\ \text{(N)} &\quad\quad \text{(kg)} \quad\quad \text{(m/s}^2\text{)} \\ F &= m \times a \end{aligned}$$

Newton's second law tells us that for a given body, the bigger the unbalanced force, the greater is the acceleration.

This law also explains why some very large articulated lorries take a long distance to stop. When the stopping force is constant, the deceleration is inversely proportional to the mass of the lorry.

Examples

1 Calculate the force needed to give a train of mass 250 000 kg an acceleration of 0.5 m/s^2.

Answer

$F = m \times a$

$= 250\,000 \times 0.5$

$= \mathbf{125\,000\,N}$

2 A forward thrust of 400 N exerted by a speedboat engine enables it to go through the water at constant velocity. The speedboat has a mass of 500 kg. Calculate the thrust required to accelerate the speedboat at 2 m/s^2.

FORCES

Answer

Note the phrase 'at constant velocity'. This is a clue to use Newton's first law. If the thrust exerted by the engine is 400 N, there must be an equal and opposite force of 400 N due to the drag of the water on the boat. To calculate the force to accelerate the speedboat you should draw a force diagram.

unbalanced force = mass × acceleration

$F - 400 = 500 \times 2$

$F - 400 = 1000$

$F = \mathbf{1400\,N}$

Summary of balanced and unbalanced forces

* Balanced forces have no effect on the movement of an object. If it is stationary it will remain stationary; if it is moving it will carry on moving at the same speed and in the same direction.
* Unbalanced forces will affect the movement of an object.
* An unbalanced force on an object causes its velocity to change – it accelerates. The greater the force, the greater the acceleration.
* The greater the mass of an object, the greater the force needed to make it accelerate.

Questions

1. A bicycle and rider have a total mass of 90 kg and travel along a horizontal road at a steady speed. The forward force exerted by the cyclist is 40 N.
   a) Explain why the cyclist does not accelerate.
   b) The rider increases the forward force to 70 N. Calculate the acceleration.
2. Calculate the force of friction on a car of mass 1200 kg if it accelerates at 2 m/s² when the engine force is 3000 N.

3 The diagram below shows the forces on a car of mass 800 kg.

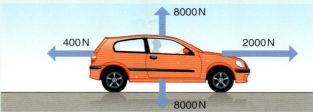

   a) In what direction will the car accelerate?
   b) Calculate the car's acceleration.

4 The blades of a helicopter exert an upward force of 25 000 N. The mass of the helicopter is 2000 kg.

   a) Calculate the weight of the helicopter.
   b) Calculate the acceleration of the helicopter.

5 A forward thrust of 300 N exerted by a speedboat engine enables the speedboat to go through the water at a constant speed. The speedboat has a mass of 500 kg.
   Calculate the thrust required to accelerate the speedboat at 2 m/s^2.

6 A car of mass 1200 kg accelerates at 3 m/s^2 along a road. Calculate the forward thrust exerted by the car's engine if all resistive forces add up to 400 N.

7 A car and driver are travelling at 24 m/s and the driver decides to brake, bringing the car to rest in 8 seconds. The mass of the car and driver is 1200 kg.
   a) Calculate the deceleration of the car.
   b) Calculate the size of the unbalanced force that brings the car to rest.

8 A cyclist and her bicycle have a combined mass of 60 kg. When she cycles with a forward force of 120 N, she moves at a steady speed. However, when she cycles with a forward force of more than 120 N, she accelerates.
   a) Explain, in terms of forces, why the girl moves at a steady speed when the force is 120 N.
   b) Calculate her acceleration when the forward force is 300 N.

9 A Land Rover's brakes are applied and the vehicle's velocity changes from 50 m/s to zero in 5 seconds.
   a) Calculate the acceleration of the Land Rover.
   b) The resultant force causing this acceleration is 18 000 N. Calculate the mass of the Land Rover.

10 A car of mass 1000 kg is travelling at 20 m/s and collides with a wall. The front of the car collapses in 0.1 seconds, by which time the car is at rest.
   a) Calculate the deceleration of the car.
   b) Calculate the force exerted by the wall on the car.

FORCES

▶ Momentum

Momentum is a useful quantity to consider when cars are involved in collisions or when tennis players and golfers strike the ball.

Momentum is defined as the mass of a body multiplied by its velocity:

$$\underset{(\text{kg m/s})}{\text{momentum}} = \underset{(\text{kg})}{\text{mass}} \times \underset{(\text{m/s})}{\text{velocity}}$$

Momentum has size and direction so it is a vector quantity.

Example
Calculate the momentum of a 1.5 kg football travelling at 12 m/s.

Answer
$$\text{momentum} = \text{mass} \times \text{velocity}$$
$$= 1.5 \times 12$$
$$= \mathbf{18 \, kg \, m/s}$$

Force and momentum

If a steady force F acting on a body of mass m increases its velocity from u to v in time t, the acceleration is given by:

$$\text{acceleration} = \frac{\text{change in velocity}}{\text{time taken}}$$

$$a = \frac{v - u}{t} \quad (1)$$

In other words, the acceleration is the change in velocity per unit time. Multiplying both sides of equation (1) by mass m gives:

$$m \times a = \frac{m(v - u)}{t} \quad (2)$$

The left-hand side of equation (2) is part of Newton's second law, so clearly the right-hand side of this equation must also be an alternative version of Newton's second law:

$$F = \frac{m(v - u)}{t} \quad (3)$$

Removing the brackets from equation (3) gives:

$$F = \frac{mv - mu}{t} \quad (4)$$

Now mv is the final momentum and mu is the initial momentum of a body of mass m, so ($mv - mu$) represents the change in momentum. So equation (4) tells us that the rate of change of momentum is the size of the force. In other words:

$$\text{force} = \frac{\text{change in momentum}}{\text{time taken}} \quad (5)$$

Equation (5) is very useful when considering car crashes.

Example

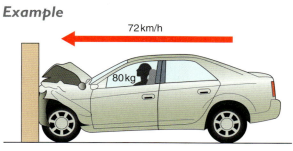

Consider a car and driver, mass 80 kg, travelling at 72 km/h (20 m/s) colliding with a wall in a time interval of 0.2 seconds.

Answer

Initial momentum $= m \times u$ 　　Final momentum $= m \times v$
　　　　　　　　$= 80 \times 20$ 　　　　　　　　　　　$= 80 \times 0$
　　　　　　　　$= 1600$ kg m/s 　　　　　　　　　$= 0$ kg m/s

Change in momentum $= 1600 - 0 = 1600$ kg m/s

According to equation (5):

$$\text{force} = \frac{\text{change in momentum}}{\text{time taken}}$$

$$= \frac{1600}{0.2}$$

$$= 8000 \text{ N}$$

The human body is not designed to withstand such a large force. How can this force be reduced?

There's not a lot the driver can do about the change in momentum apart from remembering that SPEED KILLS. However, if the time of impact with the wall were increased to, say, 4 seconds then the new force on the driver would be given by:

$$F = \frac{1600}{4}$$

$$= 400 \text{ N}$$

This is a substantial decrease, increasing the probability of the driver surviving the collision. Clearly these calculations show that the longer the time of impact, the smaller the force the driver sustains.

Crumple zones, seatbelts and air bags

Crumple zones are areas at the front and the rear of a car that are designed to collapse relatively easily and *slowly*. The car's cabin is designed to be structurally much stronger, so it does not crumple around the passengers. The cabin continues moving briefly, crushing the front of the car against the obstacle. Of course, crumple zones will only protect passengers if they move with the cabin of the car – i.e. if they are secured to the seats by seatbelts.

Look at the photo of the car in Figure 8. Notice how the front of the car has crumpled in the collision, but the passenger compartment is relatively undamaged.

Figure 8 Crumple zones make forces on car passengers smaller

FORCES

Question

11. A car is travelling at 30 km/h when it skids, leaves the road and collides with a tree.
    a) What is 30 km/h in metres per second?
    b) An air bag inflates in the collision. From the time the driver hits the air bag, it takes 0.03 s for the car to stop. What is the average acceleration?
    c) The driver has a mass of 70 kg. What is the average force on him from the air bag?

Both the front and the rear of cars are designed so that in a collision they will be crushed steadily, so slowing the car down more gradually. These crumple zones spread the collisions over a longer time and so reduce the force on the passengers and hopefully reduce injuries.

Air bags in cars give extra protection in collisions. Front air bags are fitted in the steering wheel or in the dashboard. The shock of a front-end collision sets off a chemical reaction inside the bag. The reaction forms a large volume of gas very quickly. The gas fills the bag, which holds a passenger in their seat. The bags are porous and go down quickly after the accident.

Air bags are only set off if the collision speed is over 30 km/h. Even with an air bag this would be very unpleasant!

▶ Mass and weight

In everyday life, the terms **mass** and **weight** are used interchangeably. In physics, however, we must be very careful to distinguish between the two clearly.

What is mass?

Mass is defined as *the amount of matter in a body*. Mass is measured in kilograms (kg). It is another example of a scalar quantity.

However, Newton's second law of motion allows a more exact definition to be made. In Figure 9 you can see that a more massive trolley accelerates more slowly than a less massive trolley for the same force applied. Massive objects have an in-built reluctance to start moving – this is called **inertia** (from the Latin for 'laziness').

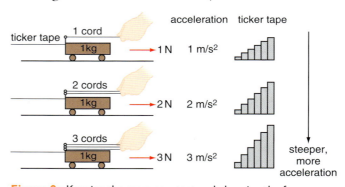

Figure 9a Keeping the mass constant and changing the force

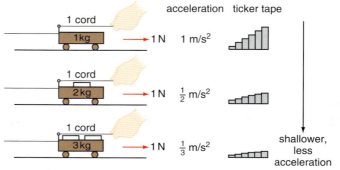

Figure 9b Keeping the force constant and changing the mass

⇨ DID YOU KNOW?

Large oil tankers turn off their engines 2 miles before reaching port.

MASS AND WEIGHT

What is weight?

Weight is a force and is a *measure of the size of the gravitational pull on an object* exerted – in our case, by the Earth. Near the surface of the Earth, there is a force of 10 N on each 1 kg of mass. We say that the Earth's **gravitational field strength**, g, is 10 N/kg.

The weight, W, of an object is the force that gravity exerts on it. The formula for weight is:

$$\begin{array}{c} \text{weight} \\ \text{(N)} \\ W \end{array} = \begin{array}{c} \text{mass} \\ \text{(kg)} \\ m \end{array} \times \begin{array}{c} \text{acceleration (due to gravity)} \\ \text{(m/s}^2\text{)} \\ g \end{array}$$

Weight is measured in newtons (N). It is a vector quantity, so it has direction as well as size.

The value of g is roughly the same everywhere on the Earth's surface. But the further you move away from the Earth, the smaller g becomes.

The Moon is smaller than the Earth and pulls objects towards it less strongly. On the Moon's surface, the value of g is 1.6 N/kg.

In deep space, far away from the planets, there are no gravitational pulls, so g is zero, and therefore everything is weightless.

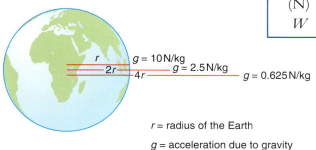

r = radius of the Earth
g = acceleration due to gravity

Figure 10 The gravitational field strength, g, decreases with distance from the Earth

➲ DID YOU KNOW?

Your weight at the Equator is slightly less than your weight at the North Pole because of the Earth's shape. If your mass was 40 kg, your weight at the North Pole would be 400 N but on the Equator it would be 397.5 N.

Example

What is the weight of a 70 kg man on:
a) the Earth, where $g = 10$ N/kg
b) the Moon, where $g = 1.6$ N/kg?

Answer

a) $W = m \times g$
$ = 70 \times 10$
$ = \mathbf{700\ N}$

b) $W = m \times g$
$ = 70 \times 1.6$
$ = \mathbf{112\ N}$

The size of g also gives the gravitational acceleration, because from Newton's second law:

$$\text{acceleration} = \frac{\text{force}}{\text{mass}}$$

$$g = \frac{F}{m}$$

So an alternative set of units for g is m/s².

Mass	Weight
Scalar	Vector
Measured in kilograms	Measured in newtons
Never varies	Varies from place to place

Table 2 Comparing mass and weight

FORCES

Questions

12 Julie said, 'My weight is 35 kg.' What is wrong with this statement and what do you think her weight really is?
13 A ball bearing is dropped gently into a tall cylinder of oil, which resists its motion. Describe what will happen to the ball bearing.
14 An astronaut standing on the surface of the Moon releases a hammer and a feather from the same height at the same time. What will happen and why?
15 Why does a parachute slow down a falling parachutist?
16 The speed–time graph below is for a parachutist. Explain the shape of each section – AB, BC, CD and DE:

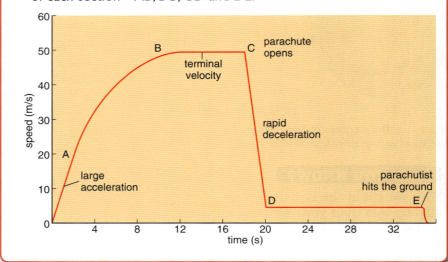

▶ Density

The spectators at a football match are densely packed on the terraces, whereas the footballers on the pitch are well spread out. In a similar way, different materials have different densities. Some materials, such as lead, have large atoms which are packed together very tightly. We say that lead is a very dense material. In contrast, polystyrene has very small, well-spaced-out atoms.

In physics, a fairer comparison between materials such as lead and polystyrene is made using the idea of **density**. The density of a material is defined as *the mass per unit volume*. It is calculated using the formula:

$$\text{density} = \frac{\text{mass}}{\text{volume}}$$

The unit of density is the kilogram per cubic metre (kg/m^3). Occasionally you will also see the unit gram per cubic centimetre (g/cm^3).

The density of lead is 11 g/cm^3, which means that a piece of lead with a volume 1 cm^3 has a mass of 11 g. Therefore 5 cm^3 of lead has a mass of 55 g.

Figure 11 Concorde is made from aluminium to give it low density and high strength

DENSITY

DID YOU KNOW?
The Earth is the densest planet in our Solar System.

Substance	Density in g/cm³	Density in kg/m³
Aluminium	2.7	2 700
Iron	8.9	8 900
Gold	19.3	19 300
Pure water	1.0	1 000
Ice	0.9	900
Petrol	0.8	800
Mercury	13.6	13 600
Hydrogen	0.00009	0.09
Air	0.0013	1.3

Table 3 The densities of some common substances

Knowing the density of a substance, the mass of any volume of that substance can be calculated. This enables engineers to work out the mass (and hence weight) of a structure if they know from the plans the volumes of the materials to be used and their densities.

Example
Taking the density of mercury as 14 g/cm³, find:
a) the mass of 7 cm³ of mercury
b) the volume of 42 g of mercury.

Answer

a) $d = \dfrac{m}{V}$

$14 = \dfrac{m}{7}$

$m = 14 \times 7$

$= 98 \text{ g}$

b) $d = \dfrac{m}{V}$

$14 = \dfrac{42}{V}$

$V = \dfrac{42}{14}$

$= 3 \text{ cm}^3$

Measuring density

To determine the density of a substance we need to measure its mass and its volume. The density, d, will then be given by the ratio of its mass (m) to its volume (V).

Regularly-shaped object

The mass of such an object is measured using a top-pan balance, and the volume by measuring its dimensions with a ruler and using the appropriate formula. For example:

* volume of a rectangular block = length × breadth × height
* volume of a circular cylinder = π × radius² × height

Irregularly-shaped object

If the shape of the object is too irregular for the volume to be determined using formulae, then a displacement method is used as shown in Figure 12. As before, the mass is measured using a top-pan balance and the density calculated as outlined previously.

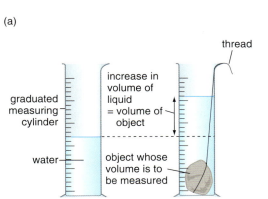

Figure 12a The volume of a small object can be measured in a measuring cylinder

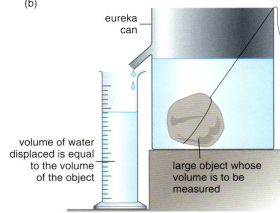

b Measuring the volume of a large object requires a eureka can

Liquid

In this method, you first measure the mass of a dry, empty, graduated cylinder. The liquid under test is then poured into the cylinder and its volume is measured – the mass of the cylinder and liquid is then measured (Figure 13).

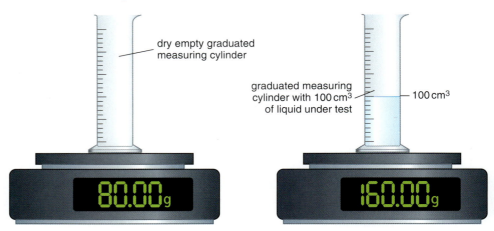

Figure 13 Measuring the density of a liquid

The mass of the specified volume of liquid is determined by subtracting the mass of the empty cylinder from the combined mass of cylinder and liquid. The density of the liquid is found as before, by dividing the mass of the liquid by its volume.

Explaining the variation in density of solids, liquids and gases using the kinetic theory

There are three states of matter – **solids**, **liquids and gases**. Matter is made up of molecules in constant motion.

In **solids**, molecules are **packed very close together**. They vibrate about fixed positions and have strong forces of attraction between them. As a result, solids have a high density.

In **liquids** the molecules are **close together** but not as close as they are in solids. They can move around in any direction and are not fixed in position. The forces of attraction between them are still quite strong but, again, not as strong as in solids. Liquids have a medium density.

In **gases** the molecules are very far apart with **large distances between them**. They move around very quickly in all directions and the forces of attraction between them are very, very weak. Gases have a very low density.

Generally when solids are heated their density decreases as the intermolecular spacing increases. Similarly, when liquids evaporate the density decreases as the average spacing between molecules increases significantly.

Questions

17 Consult Table 3 on page 23 to find which substance, of mass 57.9 g, has a volume of 3 cm^3.

CIRCULAR MOTION

18 Aluminium has a density of 2.7 g/cm³.
  a) What is the mass of 20 cm³ of aluminium?
  b) What is the volume of 54 g of aluminium?

19 A piece of steel of mass 120 g has a volume of 15 cm³. Calculate its density.

20 Calculate the mass of air in a room with the dimensions 10 m by 5 m by 3 m, if air has a density of 1.26 kg/m³.

21 A stone of mass 60 g is lowered into a measuring cylinder causing the liquid level to rise from 15 cm³ to 35 cm³. Calculate the density of the stone in g/cm³.

22 The capacity of a petrol tank in a saloon car is 0.08 m³. Calculate the mass of petrol in a full tank if the density of petrol is 800 kg/m³.

23 The mass of an evacuated steel container, of volume 1000 cm³, is 350 g. The mass of the steel container when full of air is 351.2 g. Calculate the density of air.

24 100 identical copper rivets are put into an empty measuring cylinder and 50 cm³ of water is poured over them.
  What is the volume of:
  a) the 100 copper rivets
  b) one copper rivet?
  c) If all the copper rivets together have a mass of 180 g, calculate the density of copper.

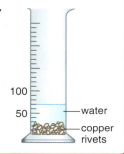

▶ Circular motion

There are many examples of circular motion:

* planets going round the Sun
* the Moon orbiting the Earth
* clothes in a tumble drier
* a car turning a corner, the shape of which may follow an arc of a circle.

Figure 14 These are all examples of circular motion

Why do bodies move in a circular path?

Consider a ball attached to a string being whirled around in a horizontal circle (Figure 15).

It is clear that the direction of motion is constantly changing. At A it points along the tangent at A up the page, whereas at C it points along the tangent down the page.

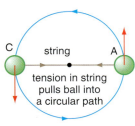

Figure 15 This ball is moving in a circular path, but what would happen if the string broke?

25

As we learned earlier in this chapter, velocity has both size and direction but speed has only size. Velocity is speed in a specified direction and if the direction of a moving body changes, even if its speed does not, then its velocity has changed.

According to its definition, acceleration is the change of velocity in unit time, and so during its whirling motion, the ball is accelerating.

It follows from Newton's first law of motion that if we consider a body moving in a circle to be accelerating, then there must be a force acting on it to cause the acceleration. In the case of the whirling ball, it must be the tension in the string pulling inwards on the ball which causes the velocity of the ball to change its direction at every point in its path.

Investigating the factors affecting the centripetal force

A larger force is needed if:

* the speed of the ball is increased
* the radius of the circle is decreased
* the mass of the ball is increased.

The first two points follow directly from Newton's second law: $F = ma$. If the force is bigger than the string can bear, the string breaks – so what will happen to the ball?

According to Newton's first law, the body will continue in its state of uniform motion – the ball will fly off at a tangent to the point where the ball is when the string breaks. It will not fly radially outwards – this is a common misconception.

The force that acts towards the centre and keeps a body in a circular path is called the **centripetal** (centre-seeking) **force**. We say that the tension in the string provides the centripetal force. In Figure 16, gravitational attraction between the Earth and Moon provides the centripetal force.

In Figure 17, the electrostatic force of attraction between the proton and the electron in the hydrogen atom provides the centripetal force.

In Figure 18, the friction force between the tyres of a car and the road provide the centripetal force.

Figure 16 The Moon experiences a centripetal force as it orbits the Earth

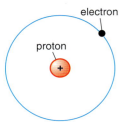

Figure 17 An electron experiences a centripetal force as it orbits a nucleus

Figure 18 A rally car experiences a centripetal force as it turns a corner

▶ Moments

Moment of a force

Door handles are usually placed as far away from the hinges as possible so that the door can be opened and closed easily. A much larger force would be needed if the handle was near the hinges. Similarly, it is easier to tighten or loosen a nut with a long spanner than with a short one.

The **turning effect** or **moment** of a force depends on two factors:

* the size of the force
* the distance the force is from the turning point or **pivot**.

(Occasionally you may see the word 'fulcrum' which is the old English word for pivot.)

MOMENTS

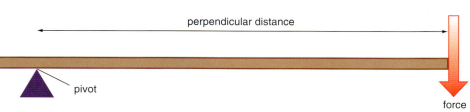

Figure 19 Calculating the moment of a force

The moment of a force is measured by multiplying the force by the perpendicular distance (the distance at right angles) of the line of action of the force from the pivot. This can be written as:

moment of a force = force × perpendicular distance from the pivot

When the force is measured in newtons (N) and the distance from the pivot is measured in metres (m), the unit of the moment of a force is the newton metre (N m).

DID YOU KNOW?
Archimedes claimed that he could lift the Earth! He maintained that if he had a very long lever pivoted on the Atlas Mountains, he could quite easily lift the Earth.

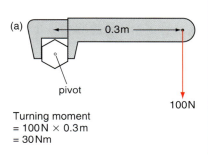

Turning moment
= 100 N × 0.3 m
= 30 Nm

Example
Find the moment of a 100 N force applied at a perpendicular distance of 0.3 m from the centre of a nut.

Answer
Turning moment = force × perpendicular distance
= 100 × 0.3
= **30 N m**

Investigating the principle of moments
The **principle of moments** can be investigated using the following method.

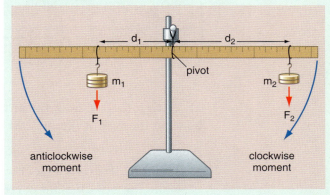

Figure 20 Experiment to investigate the principle of moments

* Suspend and balance a metre ruler at the 50 cm mark using twine.
* Adjust the position of the twine so that the rule does not rotate.
* Hang unequal masses, m_1 and m_2 (100 g slotted masses), from either side of the metre ruler as shown in Figure 20.
* Adjust the position of the masses until the metre ruler is balanced (in equilibrium) again.

* Gravity exerts forces F_1 and F_2 on the masses m_1 and m_2. Remember that a 100 g slotted mass is equivalent to 1 N. Record the results in a table like this and repeat for other loads and distances.

m_1 (g)	F_1 (N)	d_1 (cm)	$F_1 \times d_1$ (N cm)	m_2 (g)	F_2 (N)	d_2 (cm)	$F_2 \times d_2$ (N cm)

* The force F_1 is trying to turn the metre ruler anticlockwise, and its moment is $F_1 \times d_1$. F_2 is trying to turn the metre ruler clockwise – its moment is $F_2 \times d_2$.
* When the metre ruler is balanced (i.e. in equilibrium), the results should show that the anticlockwise moment $F_1 \times d_1$ equals the clockwise moment $F_2 \times d_2$.
The principle of moments is:

> When a body is in equilibrium, the sum of the clockwise moments about any point equals the sum of the anticlockwise moments about the same point.

Another very important consequence of the fact that the metre ruler is in equilibrium is that the forces acting on the stick in any direction must balance. The upward forces must balance the downward forces. This idea is very useful when doing problems.

Example
A boy, weighing 600 N, sits 6 m away from the pivot of a see-saw, as shown below.

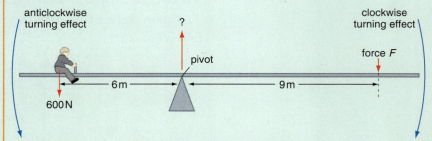

a) What force 9 m from the pivot is needed to balance the see-saw?
b) Find the size of the upward force exerted by the pivot.

Answer
a) The force F exerts a clockwise turning effect about the pivot while the boy's weight exerts an anticlockwise turning effect. Since the see-saw is balanced, we can write:

$$\text{clockwise moment} = \text{anticlockwise moment}$$
$$F \times \text{distance from pivot} = 600 \text{ N} \times \text{distance from pivot}$$
$$F \times 9 \text{ m} = 600 \text{ N} \times 6 \text{ m}$$
$$F = 600 \times \tfrac{6}{9}$$
$$= 400 \text{ N}$$

MOMENTS

> **b)** Also, since the body is balanced (in equilibrium):
>
> the upward force at the pivot = the sum of the downward forces acting on the see-saw
>
> = 400 N + 600 N
>
> = **1000 N**

Questions

25 The diagram shows a car park barrier. The weight of the barrier is 150 N and its centre of mass is 0.9 m from the pivot.

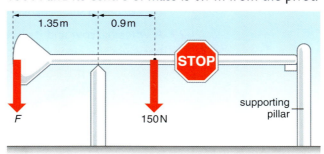

a) Calculate the size of the clockwise moment produced by the barrier's weight about the pivot.
b) Calculate the size of the force, F, on the left of the pivot which will just lift the barrier off the supporting pillar.

26 A uniform metre ruler is pivoted at its midpoint. A load of 4 N acts on the right-hand side at a distance of 36 cm from the pivot.

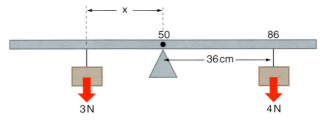

Calculate the distance from the pivot where you would place a 3 N weight to balance the metre ruler.

27 The diagram below shows a plan view of a gate pivoted at C. The boy at A is pushing on the gate with a force of 100 N and a man at B is pushing in the opposite direction so that the gate does not move.

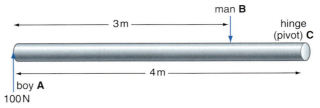

a) Calculate the moment of the force exerted by the boy about C.
b) What is the moment of the force exerted by the man about C?
c) What size of force is exerted by the man?

FORCES

28 The centre of mass (see below) of an 80 cm snooker cue is 15 cm from its thick end.

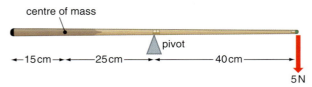

The cue balances on a pivot 40 cm from its thick end when a force of 5 N is applied to the thin area.

a) Calculate the moment of the 5 N force about the pivot and state the direction in which it acts.

b) Calculate the weight of the snooker cue.

29 A wheelbarrow and its load together weigh 600 N. The distance between the pivot and the wheelbarrow's centre of mass is 75 cm.

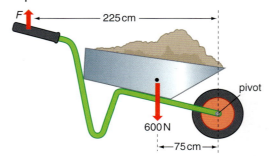

The distance between the handles and the pivot is 225 cm. Calculate the size of the smallest force, F, needed to lift the wheelbarrow at the handles.

30 The diagram shows a side view of a uniform paving slab of weight 100 N.

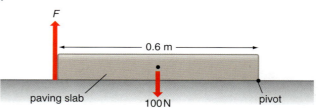

Calculate the smallest force, F, needed to lift the paving slab.

▶ Centre of gravity and stability

All objects have a point at which we can consider all their weight to be concentrated. This point is referred to as the **centre of gravity** – sometimes called the **centre of mass** of the object.

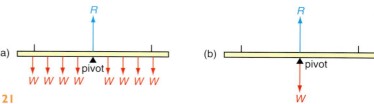

Figure 21

CENTRE OF GRAVITY AND STABILITY

Figure 21 shows a metre ruler that is balanced about its midpoint. You could imagine the metre ruler as consisting of a series of 10 cm sections. The mass of each section is pulled towards the centre of the Earth by the force of gravity, so there are several small forces acting on the metre ruler. It is possible to replace all of these forces by a single resultant force acting through its centre of gravity, G. This force may be balanced by the reaction exerted by the pivot, as shown in Figure 21b.

The centre of gravity can be thought of as the point of balance. If a body has a regular shape, such as a flat disc or a rectangular sheet of metal, then its centre of gravity is at its geometrical centre.

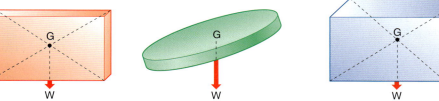

Figure 22 Working out the centre of gravity for regular objects

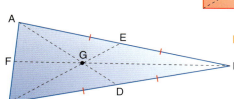

Figure 23 Where the medians intersect is the triangle's centre of gravity

Flat triangular shapes are a little more difficult. In such cases, lines called **medians** are drawn from the corners of the triangle to the midpoints of the opposite sides – where the medians intersect is the centre of gravity.

To find the centre of gravity of an irregularly-shaped lamina

A **lamina** is a body, the shape of which is in the form of a flat thin sheet.

For this experiment, it is important to realise that when a body is suspended so that it can swing freely, it will come to rest with its centre of gravity vertically below the point of suspension.

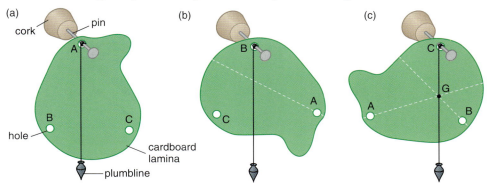

Figure 24 To find the centre of gravity of an irregular lamina

The stages involved in this investigation are:

* Hang an irregularly-shaped sheet of cardboard from a pin, embedded in a cork.
* Hang a plumb-line from the same pin.
* When the cardboard settles, mark the vertical line with a pencil.
* Repeat from two further points.

The intersection of the vertical lines from the three points of suspension will fix the centre of gravity.

FORCES

Equilibrium and stability

A body is in **equilibrium** when both the resultant force and resultant turning effect on it are zero. There are three types of equilibrium which are determined by what happens to the object when it is given a small push.

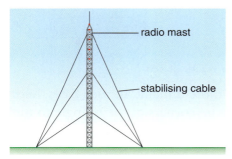

Figure 25 This ball is in neutral equilibrium with the ground

* A ball on a flat piece of ground is in **neutral equilibrium**. When given a gentle push, the ball rolls, keeping its centre of gravity at the same height above the point of contact with the ground.
* A tall radio mast is in **unstable equilibrium**. It is balanced with its centre of gravity above its base, but a small push from the wind will move its centre of gravity downwards. To prevent the mast toppling, it is stabilised with cables.
* A car on the road is in **stable equilibrium** (Figure 27a). If the car is tilted (b) the centre of gravity is lifted. In this position, the action of the weight keeps the car on the road. In (c) the centre of gravity lies above the wheels, so the car is in a position of unstable equilibrium. If the car tips further (d) the weight provides a turning effect to turn the car over. Cars with a low centre of gravity and a wide wheelbase are the most stable on the road.

Figure 26 This radio mast is in unstable equilibrium

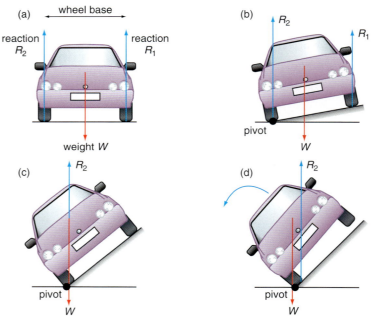

Figure 27 As the car tilts further, it becomes more and more unstable until at position (d), it topples over

Figure 28 This racing car is extremely stable because of its low centre of gravity and wide wheelbase

Questions

31 The diagrams represent thin sheets of plastic.

  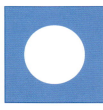

   a) Copy the diagrams and draw construction lines to show where the centre of gravity of each plastic sheet is.

   b) The central circular portion of the square on the right has been cut out. If the centre of the circle is at the centre of the square, where will the centre of gravity of this plastic sheet be?

32 a) What is meant by the 'centre of gravity' of an object?

   b) The diagram shows a pencil with a penknife attached balancing on its point.

   i) Explain why this happens.

   ii) What would happen if the knife blade were closed slightly?

   c) This diagram shows a piece of cardboard. Copy the diagram exactly and mark a possible position for the centre of gravity.

33 The diagram shows a racing car.

   a) Sketch the diagram and mark with a cross the approximate position of the centre of gravity.

   b) What two features of the car give it great stability?

34 The diagrams show two drinking glasses.

   a) Copy the diagrams and mark with a cross the approximate position of the centre of gravity of each glass.

   b) Which glass is likely to be more stable?

   c) Give two reasons for your answer to part **b)**.

35 a) The diagram shows a solid cone in stable equilibrium.

Draw two further diagrams to illustrate a solid cone in:
i) unstable equilibrium
ii) neutral equilibrium.

b) These diagrams show two similarly-shaped table lamps, A and B. The bases are solid.

A   B

i) Copy the diagrams and mark with a cross where you might expect the centre of gravity of each lamp to be.
ii) Which lamp is likely to be more stable?
iii) Give two reasons for your answer to part ii).

36 a) The diagram shows a T-shaped lamina, in which QR is twice as long as AB.

Copy the diagram and mark on it:
i) a dot labelled X – the centre of gravity of the rectangle ABCD
ii) a dot labelled Y – the centre of gravity of the rectangle PQRS
iii) a dot labelled Z – the approximate position of the centre of gravity of the whole shape.

b) Sketch the shape of a lamina in which the centre of gravity falls outside the shape itself. Mark on the sketch approximately where the centre of gravity lies.

Search
- terminal velocity
- braking distance
- density
- friction
- principle of moments
- circular motion

Exam questions

1 a) Explain what is meant by 'density'. *(2 marks)*

b) Describe briefly how you could use a measuring cylinder half filled with water to find the volume of a bracelet. In your description, state what measurements you would make and what calculation you would carry out. *(4 marks)*

c) A certain bracelet has a volume of 2.4 cm³ and a mass of 46 g. Calculate its density. Show clearly how you get your answer. *(3 marks)*

d) The bracelet is made from a metal which is almost 100% pure. Use your answer to part **c)** and the table below to find out what the metal is. *(1 mark)*

Metal	Copper	Gold	Lead	Platinum
Density in g/cm³	8.9	19.3	11.3	21.5

2 a) Data relating to a particular concrete slab are given below.

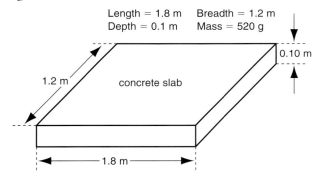

Length = 1.8 m   Breadth = 1.2 m
Depth = 0.1 m   Mass = 520 g

i) Use the data in the table to calculate the volume of this concrete slab. Show clearly how you get your answer. *(4 marks)*

ii) For bridge construction, the concrete slabs must have a density of at least 2350 kg/m³. Is this particular slab dense enough to be used for bridge construction? Show clearly how you get your answer. *(4 marks)*

b) i) Explain what is meant by the 'centre of gravity' of an object. *(1 mark)*

The diagram below shows a wheelbarrow at rest on level ground. The weight of the wheelbarrow and its contents is 1500 N.

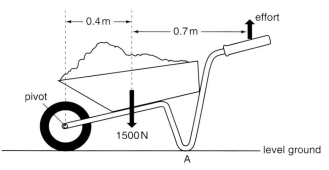

ii) Use the values on the diagram to calculate the moment of the 1500 N force about the pivot. Show clearly how you get your answer. *(5 marks)*

iii) Use your answer to part **b) ii)** to calculate the effort that must be applied to the handles, if the wheelbarrow is just to lift off the ground at A. Show clearly how you get your answer. *(4 marks)*

iv) What is the upward vertical reaction (supporting force) from the ground through the pivot, when the wheelbarrow is just lifted off the ground by the effort? Show clearly how you get your answer. *(2 marks)*

3 Energy

▶ Energy forms

It is important to understand the difference between **energy forms** and **energy resources**. Energy forms are the different ways in which energy can appear – such as heat energy, light energy and chemical energy. Energy resources are the different ways of supplying a particular energy form. Table 1 summarises some of the main energy forms.

Energy form	Definition	Examples of resources
Chemical	The energy stored in a substance that is released on burning	Coal, oil, natural gas, peat (turf), wood, food
Gravitational potential	The energy a body contains as a result of its height above the ground	Stored energy in the dam (reservoir) of a hydroelectric power station
Kinetic	The energy of a moving object	Wind, waves, tides
Nuclear	The energy stored in the nucleus of an atom	Uranium, plutonium

Table 1 Forms of energy

Common energy forms are **heat**, **light**, **sound**, **electrical**, **magnetic** and **strain potential**. The last of these is the energy a body has when it has been stretched or squeezed out of shape and will return to its original shape when the force is removed – like a wind-up toy.

One of the fundamental laws of physics is the **law of conservation of energy**. This states that:

> Energy can neither be created nor destroyed, but it can change its form.

We can show energy changes in an **energy flow diagram**.

What energy changes take place when we strike a match?

What energy changes take place when we stretch a catapult?

What energy changes take place when we ring an electric bell?

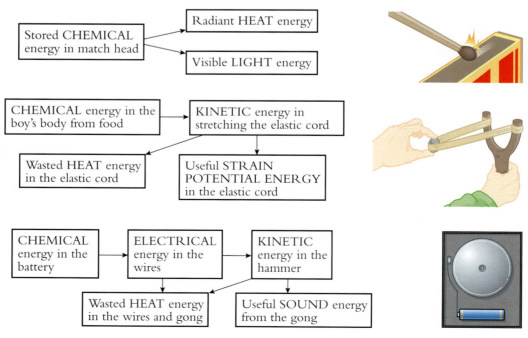

36

ENERGY RESOURCES

Energy flow diagrams are a useful way of showing the main energy changes taking place, but they have two major **limitations**. They usually:

* do not show ALL the energy transformations taking place
* do not show the amount of energy being changed from one form to another.

▶ Energy resources

Energy resources can be classified in several different ways. One is to split them into renewable and non-renewable resources. **Renewable resources** are those that are replaced by nature in less than a human lifetime. **Non-renewable resources** are those that are used faster than they can be replaced by nature.

The Government has said that 15% of our electrical energy must come from renewable resources by 2020. However, in 2010, the Government admitted that 'the current rate of growth of renewable energy in the UK is too slow to meet European Union targets for 15 per cent of energy to come from renewable sources by 2020.' (*The Ecologist*, July 2010)

> **DID YOU KNOW?**
>
> In 2010, the Government said it ruled out using taxpayers' money to build the 10 mile tidal barrage across the Severn Estuary, claiming that research and development cash could be better spent on energy projects elsewhere. The project would have cost £20 billion and would have generated 5% of Britain's electrical energy.

Renewable resource	Comment
Solar cells	Solar cells convert sunlight (**solar energy**) directly into electricity. Solar cells are joined together into **solar arrays**.
Hydroelectric power stations	Because of its height from the ground, water in a dam (reservoir) contains **gravitational potential energy**. The water is allowed to fall from the dam through a pipe, and it gains **kinetic energy** as it falls. The fast-flowing water falls on a **turbine**, which drives a **generator**. The output from the generator is **electrical energy**. Some **hydroelectric power stations** use **pumped storage** reservoirs. At times of low demand, such as in the early hours of the morning, the power station buys cheap electricity and uses it to pump water up to a high reservoir. During the day, when demand is high, they sell the electricity they produce at a higher price.
Tidal barrages	A **tidal barrage** is created when a dam is built across a river estuary. As the tide rises and falls every 12 hours, provided the water levels on each side of the dam are not equal, water will flow through a gate in the dam. The moving water drives a turbine, which is made to turn a generator. The output from the generator is electrical energy.

Table 2 Renewable sources of energy

Renewable resource	Comment
Wave machines	Waves are produced largely by the action of the wind on the surface of water. The **wave machine** floats on the surface of the water and the up and down motion of the water forces air to drive a turbine, and so produces electricity.
Wind turbines	As the wind blows, the large blades turn and this drives a turbine. The turbine drives a generator, which produces electricity. Large numbers of turbines are often grouped together to form a **wind farm**.
Geothermal energy	**Geothermal power stations** use heat from the hot rocks deep inside the Earth. Cold water is passed down a pipe to the rocks. The water is heated by these rocks and the hot water or steam is pumped to the surface. **Geothermal energy** is often used to save fossil fuels in power stations or in district heating schemes.
Biomass	Fast-growing trees, like willow, are grown on poor-quality land (or land set aside from food production) and the timber is harvested around every 3 years. The wood is dried and turned into woodchips which are then burned in power stations to produce electricity or sold for solid fuel heating. In Brazil, biomass crops are fermented to produce **alcohol**. The alcohol is added to petrol as a way of extending the life of scarce fossil fuels. The product is called **gasohol**. Other forms of biomass include oilseed rape. The oil from the seeds is converted into **biodiesel** for road transport.

Table 2 Renewable sources of energy (continued)

DID YOU KNOW?

The Dinorwig pumped-storage hydroelectric power station in Wales uses as much water in 90 minutes as London uses in 24 hours. Because it is in Snowdonia, an area of exceptional natural beauty, all electricity cables from the station are underground, rather than hanging from pylons.

Non-renewable resource	Comment
Fossil fuels – coal, oil, natural gas	The fuel is burned in a power station to produce steam, which drives a turbine. The turbine turns a generator to produce electricity.
Nuclear power stations (uranium fission)	Uranium nuclei in a reactor split into lighter nuclei (**nuclear fission**) with the release of very large amounts of kinetic energy. This is used to produce steam, which drives a turbine. The turbine turns a generator to produce electricity.

Table 3 Non-renewable sources of energy

Advantages and disadvantages of using the different energy resources to generate electricity

Energy resource	Advantages	Disadvantages	Other comments
Fossil fuels – coal, oil, natural gas, lignite, turf	* Relatively cheap to start up * Moderately expensive to run * Large world reserves of coal (much less for other fossil fuels)	* All fossil fuels are non-renewable * All fossil fuels release carbon dioxide on burning and so contribute to global warming * Burning coal and oil also releases sulphur dioxide gas, which causes acid rain	* Coal releases the most carbon dioxide and natural gas the least per unit of electricity produced * Removing sulphur or sulphur dioxide is very expensive and adds greatly to the cost of electricity production
Nuclear fuels – mainly uranium	* Do not produce carbon dioxide * Do not emit gases that cause acid rain	* The waste products will remain dangerously radioactive for tens of thousands of years * As yet, no one has found an acceptable method to store these materials cheaply, safely and securely for such a long time * Nuclear fission fuels are non-renewable * An accident could release dangerous radioactive material which would contaminate a very wide area, leaving it unusable for decades	* Nuclear fuel is relatively cheap on world markets * Nuclear power station construction costs are much higher than fossil fuel stations, because of the need to take expensive safety precautions * Decommissioning nuclear power stations is a particularly long and expensive procedure, requiring specialist equipment and personnel
Wind farms	* A renewable energy resource * Low running costs * Conserve fossil fuels	Wind farms are: * unreliable * unsightly * very noisy * hazardous to birds	* Wind farms take up much more ground per unit of electricity produced than conventional power stations
Waves	* A renewable energy resource * Low running costs * Conserve fossil fuels	Wave generators at sea are: * unreliable * unsightly * hazardous to shipping	* Many turbines are needed to produce a substantial amount of electricity
Tides	* A renewable energy resource * Low running costs * Conserve fossil fuels	Tidal barrages are built across river estuaries and can cause: * navigation problems for shipping * destruction of habitats for wading birds and the mud-living organisms on which they feed	* Tides (unlike wind and waves) are predictable, but they vary from day to day and month to month. This makes them unsuitable for producing a constant daily amount of electrical energy

Table 4 Comparison of different energy resources

ENERGY

> **DID YOU KNOW?**
>
> According to some scientists, worldwide carbon dioxide emissions have increased from about 21.6 billion tonnes in 1995 to over 27 billion tonnes in 2005 ... and the figure is still rising!

> **DID YOU KNOW?**
>
> German people are encouraged to install arrays of solar cells on the roof of their homes to produce electricity. Germans can sell the energy to the electricity supplier for about 30 pence a unit. They can then buy the electricity for domestic use at about 10 pence per unit. So the more electricity they can make from solar cells, the less money they have to pay in their bill. But there is a catch – the pay-back time for an array of solar cells is about 20 years!

The Government thinks it would be best to invest taxpayers' money in technology to capture carbon dioxide emissions from power stations and industrial sites – an area where Britain stands to be a world leader. It believes that building wind farms and so on should be left to private companies and individuals. What is your opinion?

Ireland's natural fuel resources

Ireland has almost no coal or oil resources. The island is rich in turf (peat), but it is important not to over-exploit these resources industrially because of the damage that can be done to habitats. Ireland does, however, have an important fossil fuel resource – natural gas from the Celtic Sea. Northern Ireland has another resource – lignite. This is sometimes called **brown coal** because it is rocky like coal, but brown like peat. There are millions of tonnes of lignite reserves around Crumlin and under Lough Neagh.

Questions

1. Most of Ireland's energy needs are supplied by fossil fuels. Name three fossil fuels.
2. Which of these are energy forms?
   sound   pressure   force   weight   electricity   heat
3. Which of these six energy resources are renewable?
   gas   hydroelectricity   oil   coal   wind   tides
4. A model aircraft has its wings covered with solar panels to drive the propellers and to charge a battery. Copy and complete the following sentences to show the energy changes that take place in such an aircraft:
   The solar cells change ____ energy into ____ energy. The battery stores ____ energy. As the propellers turn they change ____ energy into useful ____ energy. As the model aircraft gains height, it gains ____ energy. The model aircraft crashes into the ground. As it does so, it produces wasted heat and ____ energy.
5. Explain what is meant by a 'renewable' energy resource.
6. In what ways is the production of electricity in a fossil fuel power station and in a nuclear power station similar? In what ways are these power stations different?
7. Nuclear waste is currently vitrified (turned into a type of glass), stored in strong metal drums and kept deep underground. Why is this an unsatisfactory long-term solution?
8. Name the polluting gas that contributes to global warming, produced by burning fossil fuels.
9. Norway has complained that Britain is partly responsible for the destruction of the Norwegian habitat by acid rain. How might this have come about?
10. What are the arguments for and against installing a nuclear power station in Ireland?

11 Imagine you are a government scientist. Write about 100 words stating the advantages of having a nuclear power station rather than one that burns fossil fuels.

12 Why do you think Northern Ireland has not yet mined the lignite resources around Crumlin?

13 Do you think the Government's target to have 15% of our electricity production from renewable resources by 2020 is realistic? What can you and your family do to contribute?

14 Give three reasons for using wind farms to generate electricity.

15 The electricity companies say that electricity is a 'clean' fuel. Why is this statement misleading?

16 For each of the devices or situations shown below, use a flow diagram to show the main energy change that is taking place. The first has been done for you.

Device/situation	Input energy form		Useful output energy form
Microphone	sound energy	→	electrical energy
Electric smoothing iron	____ energy	→	____ energy
Loudspeaker	____ energy	→	____ energy
Coal burning in an open fire	____ energy	→	____ energy
A weight falling towards the ground	____ energy	→	____ energy
A candle flame	____ energy	→	____ energy and ____ energy
Battery-powered electric drill	____ energy →	electrical energy	→ ____ energy

DID YOU KNOW?

Nuclear fusion is the joining of light hydrogen nuclei to produce helium nuclei with the release of vast quantities of energy. The reaction temperature is over 15 000 000 °C. Fusion is the reaction that occurs in the Sun. So far, man has been unable to control fusion on Earth.

The Sun

Almost all energy resources ultimately rely on the energy of the Sun. In the case of fossil fuels, we know that these resources come from the dead remains of plants and animals laid down many millions of years ago. The plants obtained their energy from the Sun by **photosynthesis**. Herbivores ate the plants, while carnivores ate the herbivores. Under the Earth's surface, these remains slowly fossilised into coal, peat, oil and gas. But other processes also rely on the Sun's energy. Hydroelectric energy depends on the water cycle, and this process begins when water evaporates as a result of absorbing radiant energy from the Sun. Wind and waves rely on the Earth's weather, which is largely controlled by the Sun. **Only geothermal and nuclear energy do not depend directly on the energy emitted by the Sun**.

▶ Work

Work is only done when a **force** causes **movement**. So, although pushing against a wall might make a person tired, no work is done because it produces no movement. Similarly, holding a book at arm's length is doing no work. But, lifting a book from the floor and putting it on a table is doing work because we are applying a force and producing movement.

We can calculate work using the following formula:

> work done = force × distance moved in direction of force
> $W \quad = \quad F \quad \times \quad d$
> (J) (N) (m)

The units in this formula are matched. Force must *always* be measured in **newtons**, and if the distance were in cm, the work would be in N cm. If the distance were in metres, the work would be in N m. The N m occurs so often that physicists have renamed it the **joule** (J).

Doing work means spending **energy**. The more work a person does, the more energy they need – the energy used is equal to the amount of work done.

Examples

1. How much work is done when a packing case is dragged 4 m across the floor against a frictional force of 45 N? How much energy is needed?

Answer
The case moves at a steady speed, so the forward force must be the same size as the friction force. So the forward force is 45 N.

$$\begin{aligned} \text{Work done} &= F \times d \\ &= 45 \times 4 \\ &= 180\,\text{J} \end{aligned}$$

The energy needed is the same as the work done, **180 J**.

2. A crane does 1200 J of useful work when it lifts a load vertically by 60 cm.
Find the weight of the load.

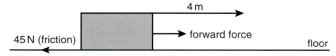

Answer
The load is being lifted, so the minimum upward force is the weight of the load.

So, $W = F \times d$
$1200 = F \times 0.6$ (remember, 60 cm is 0.6 m)
$F = \dfrac{1200}{0.6}$

So, the weight of the load is **2000 N**.

3 How much work is done by an electric motor pulling a 130 N load 6.5 m up the slope shown in the diagram if the constant tension in the string is 60 N.

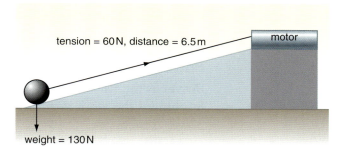

Answer
Since the tension force and distance moved are both parallel to the slope, they are both used to find the work done. The weight of the load is not needed in this question.

$$W = F \times d$$
$$= 60 \times 6.5$$
$$= \mathbf{390\,J}$$

Work and energy

Energy is the *ability* to do work. So if a machine has 500 J of stored energy, this means it can do 500 J of work. Similarly, work is sometimes thought of as the amount of energy transferred. Note that both work and energy are measured in joules.

Example
A battery stores 15 kJ of energy. If the battery is used to drive an electric motor, how high could it raise a 750 kg load if it was lifted vertically?

Answer
The battery stores 15 kJ or 15 000 J, so it can do a maximum of 15 000 J of work.

A mass of 1 kg weighs 10 N, so a mass of 750 kg has a weight of 7500 N.

So the motor must produce an upward force of at least 7500 N.

$$W = F \times d$$
$$15\,000 = 7500 \times d$$
$$d = \frac{15\,000}{7500}$$
$$= \mathbf{2\,m}$$

Note that 2 m is the *highest* that this motor could raise the load. This is because some of the energy in the battery is transformed to heat and sound. In our calculation, we have assumed that *all* the energy in the battery is used to do work against gravity.

In all calculations of this type, first write down the appropriate formula, then substitute the values you know, rearrange it if necessary, and finally carry out the calculation and give your final answer *with its unit*. Remember that showing your working is always to your benefit. If you make a mistake, the examiner can still give you credit for what you get right!

Power

Power is the *rate* of doing work. This means that the power of a machine is the work it can do in a second. The formula for calculating power is therefore:

$$\text{power} = \frac{\text{work done}}{\text{time taken}}$$

$$P = \frac{W}{t}$$

Work is measured in joules and time is measured in seconds, so power must be measured in joules per second or J/s. The J/s was renamed the **watt** in honour of James Watt, the famous Scottish engineer.

Examples

1. An electric motor is used to raise a load of 105 N. The load rises vertically 2 m in a time of 6 s. Find the work done and the power of the motor.

Answer

$$W = F \times d$$
$$= 105 \times 2$$
$$= \mathbf{210\,J}$$

$$P = \frac{W}{t}$$
$$= \frac{210}{6}$$
$$= \mathbf{35\,W}$$

2. A crane has a power of 2000 W. How much work can it do in an hour?

Answer

In power calculations, the unit of time is the second. So first convert 1 hour to seconds:

1 hour = 60 minutes = 60 × 60 seconds = 3600 seconds.

$$2000 = \frac{W}{3600}$$
$$W = 2000 \times 3600$$
$$= \mathbf{7\,200\,000\,J \text{ or } 7.2\,MJ}$$

3 A small wind generator has an average output power of 350 W. How long does it take to generate 70 kJ of electrical energy?

Answer

$$\text{energy} = 70\,000\,\text{J}$$
$$\text{power} = \frac{\text{energy}}{\text{time}}$$
$$350 = \frac{70\,000}{\text{time}}$$
$$\text{time} = \frac{70\,000}{350}$$
$$= \mathbf{200\,s}$$

4 A nail gun fires a nail with a kinetic energy of 1.8 J into a piece of wood. The average resistive force on the nail is 45 N and it stops 0.3 s after entering the wood.

Calculate:
a) the distance the nail penetrates into the wood
b) the average power of the resistive forces in stopping the nail.

Answer

a) The work done by the resistive forces
 = kinetic energy transferred = 1.8 J

$$W = F \times d$$
$$1.8 = 45 \times d$$
$$d = \frac{1.8}{45}$$
$$= \mathbf{0.04\,m\ or\ 4\,cm}$$

b) $P = \dfrac{W}{t}$

$\quad = \dfrac{1.8}{0.3}$

$\quad = \mathbf{6\,W}$

5 The photograph shows the space shuttle *Discovery* taking off.
a) The work done by the engines of the space shuttle during lift-off is 9 400 000 J. This takes the space shuttle 5 seconds. Calculate the average power generated by the engines during lift-off. Give your answer in MW.
b) One of the engines in the space shuttle exerts a force of 11 750 N. In this time interval of 5 seconds, the space shuttle rises to a height of 200 m. Calculate the work done by this engine. Give your answer in MJ.

DID YOU KNOW?

The eighteenth-century engineer James Watt wanted to sell his steam engines to mine owners. At that time, pit ponies were used underground to haul coal extensively. Watt wanted to compare the power of these ponies with the power of his engines. Comparison was necessary to convince the mine owners that his engines could do more work every hour than their ponies could. His unit of power was called the 'horsepower'. One horsepower is equivalent to about 750 watts.

ENERGY

Answer

a) $P = \dfrac{W}{t}$

$= \dfrac{9\,400\,000}{5}$

$= 1\,880\,000\,\text{W}$

$= \mathbf{1.88\,MW}$

b) $W = F \times d$

$= 11\,750 \times 200$

$= 2\,350\,000\,\text{J}$

$= \mathbf{2.35\,MJ}$

Measuring personal power

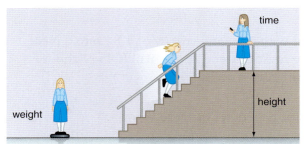

Figure 1 How to measure personal power

To measure personal power, you need to find out how long it takes you to do a given amount of work.

First, find your weight in newtons. The easy way to do this is to measure your mass in kilograms using bathroom scales, and then use the fact that 1 kg has a weight of 10 N.

Then you need to find the height of a staircase. This can be done by measuring the average height of a riser (stair) and multiplying by the number of risers in the staircase.

Finally, you need to have someone who will time you as you run up the stairs! Below are some typical results.

Measurements	
Mass of student in kg	45
Weight of student in N	450
Height of risers in cm	14.0, 13.8, 13.8, 14.0, 13.9
Average riser height in cm	13.9
Number of risers	30
Staircase height	13.9 × 30 = 417 cm = 4.17 m
Time to run upstairs in s	5.0
Calculations	
Work done	work = force × distance = 450 × 4.17 = 1876.5 J
Power	power = work ÷ time = 1876.5 ÷ 5.0 = 375.3 W

This figure of 375 W is typical of an average GCSE student. But note that the student could not keep up this power for more than a few seconds. In fact, the average adult has a sustained power of only about 75 W.

Measuring the output power of a small motor

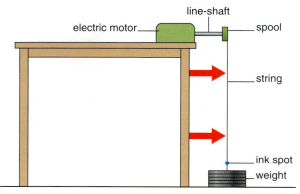

Figure 2

In this experiment, a small electric motor is connected to a line-shaft and spool. When the motor is switched on, the line-shaft rotates and, as the spool turns, the attached string rises and pulls up a known weight at a steady speed. The input voltage to the motor is kept constant.

A blob of ink is marked on the string close to the weight and two cardboard pointers are attached to the leg of the bench. The distance, h, between the two cardboard pointers is measured with a metre ruler – a suitable distance is between 1 m and 2 m.

The motor is switched on and the weight starts to rise. As the blob of ink passes the lower cardboard pointer, a stopwatch is started. As it passes the upper pointer the stopwatch is stopped. In this way, the time taken for the weight to rise through the known distance, h, is measured.

Typical results are shown in the table below.

Weight in N	Height, h in m	Work done in J	Time taken 1 in s	Time taken 2 in s	Time taken 3 in s	Average time in s	Average power in W
9.0	1.8	16.2	5.4	5.5	5.3	5.4	3.0
10.0	1.8	18.0	5.6	5.6	5.6	5.6	3.2
11.0	1.8	19.8	6.0	6.1	5.9	6.0	3.3
12.0	1.8	21.6	6.5	6.5	6.5	6.5	3.3
13.0	1.8	23.4	7.3	7.5	7.1	7.3	3.2

Table 5 Typical results for a small motor

Note that the power of the motor is not constant – over a range of increasing weights, it tends to rise and fall. This apparatus lends itself to a GCSE practical investigation into how the output power of the motor changes with the weight it lifts.

Validity of data

Data are only **valid** if the measurements taken are affected by a **single independent variable** only. Data are not valid if, for example, a **fair test** is not carried out or there is observer bias. In this case, there is only one independent variable, the weight being lifted by the motor, and the test is fair. The height and the input voltage are constant; they are controlled variables to ensure that the test is fair.

There should be no cause here to suspect observer bias. But, just to be sure, professional scientists like to repeat each other's experiments to check that they get similar results.

Reliability of data

To ensure the results are **reliable**, the experiment is repeated several times and the average power is determined for different weights.

▶ Efficiency

Efficiency is a way of describing how good a device is at transferring energy from one form to another in an intended way.

If a light bulb is rated at 100 W, this means that it normally uses 100 J of electrical energy every second. But it might only produce 5 J of light energy every second. The other 95 J is wasted as heat. This means that only 5% of the energy is transferred from electrical energy into light energy – therefore, this light bulb has an efficiency of 0.05 or 5%. If the same light bulb were used as a heater, its efficiency would be 95% – the intended output energy form would be heat, not light.

Efficiency is defined by:

$$\text{efficiency} = \frac{\text{useful energy output}}{\text{total energy input}}$$

Because efficiency is a ratio, it has no units. By the principle of the conservation of energy, energy cannot be created, so the useful energy output can never be greater than the total energy input. However, energy is wasted in *every* physical process, so the efficiency of a machine is *always* less than 1.

> ### Examples
>
> **1** An electric kettle is rated 2500 W – it produces 2500 J of heat energy every second. The kettle takes 160 seconds to boil some water, and during this time 360 000 J of heat energy pass into the water. Calculate the kettle's efficiency.
>
> ### Answer
> useful energy output (passed into water) = 360 000 J
> total energy input = 2500 × 160 = 400 000 J
>
> $$\text{efficiency} = \frac{\text{useful energy output}}{\text{total energy input}}$$
>
> $$= \frac{360\,000}{400\,000}$$
>
> $$= 0.9$$
>
> So:
>
> * 90% of the electrical energy is used to boil the water
> * 10% of the energy supplied is wasted – most will be passed through the kettle as wasted heat to the surrounding air. A small amount of heat will be lost as some water evaporates.
>
> **2** A motor rated 40 W lifts a load of 80 N to a height of 90 cm in 4 s. Find its efficiency.
>
> ### Answer
> useful energy output = work done by motor
> = force × distance
> = 80 × 0.9
> = 72 J
>
> $$\text{power} = \frac{\text{energy supplied}}{\text{time taken}}$$
>
> $$40 = \frac{\text{energy supplied}}{4}$$
>
> energy supplied = 40 × 4
> = 160 J
>
> $$\text{efficiency} = \frac{\text{useful energy output}}{\text{total energy input}}$$
>
> $$= \frac{72}{160}$$
>
> $$= 0.45$$

> **DID YOU KNOW?**
>
> In the nineteenth and twentieth centuries, many people tried to make 'perpetual motion' machines. The creators hoped that these machines would work forever without the continued addition of energy. Sadly, they did not take friction into account. Friction can never be completely eliminated and always causes waste heat and/or sound. As a result, all perpetual motion machines are doomed to fail.

GRAVITATIONAL POTENTIAL ENERGY

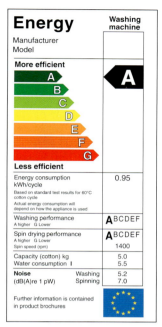

Figure 3 European Union energy efficiency label for a particular brand of washing machine

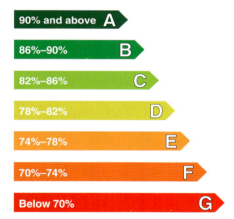

Figure 4 SEDBUK boiler efficiency range

Energy efficiency in domestic appliances

Almost every domestic electrical appliance in the United Kingdom now has an energy efficiency label. The energy efficiency label is an energy evaluation scale used by the European Union to promote energy-saving electrical appliances. This energy label must be attached and clearly visible in the front or on the top of each electrical item.

The evaluation scale gives information about the energy consumption of that electrical item. It is organised into classes from A to G, where A represents the best products (low energy consumption, very efficient) and G the worst (high energy consumption, not very efficient).

If you buy a new central heating boiler in Britain today, it will probably carry a SEDBUK label. SEDBUK stands for 'seasonal efficiency of domestic boilers in the UK'. This rating system was created by the Government to provide more accurate energy efficiency ratings for boilers.

Previously, boilers were graded using only their manufacturer's laboratory tests. However, since the introduction of the SEDBUK system, boiler ratings have become more precise, simple and consistent. A SEDBUK rating gives a boiler's **average efficiency over a typical year**.

SEDBUK ratings are categorised from A to G – with A representing the highest efficiency of over 90%, and G being the lowest, below 70%.

Do you think knowing **the average efficiency over a typical year** is more useful than a number giving the boiler's efficiency when it is sold? Why?

There are now many energy-efficiency rating schemes. One is the BFRC rating for double glazing. Type 'BFRC' into your favourite search engine and see what its label looks like.

▶ Gravitational potential energy

When any object with mass is lifted, work is done on it against the force of **gravity**. The greater the mass of the object and the higher it is lifted, the more work has to be done. The work that is done is only possible because some energy has been used. This energy is stored in the object as **gravitational potential energy**.

$$\text{Gravitational potential energy} = \text{mass} \times \text{gravity} \times \text{height} = mgh$$

where m is the mass in kg, g is the gravitational field strength in N/kg and h is the vertical height in m.

When the object is released, it falls back to Earth and the stored energy can be recovered. If the object crashes into the ground, a bang (sound energy) is heard and heat is produced.

ENERGY

In both CCEA Science: Double Award and GCSE Science: Physics examinations it is important to **remember** that a mass of 1 kg has a weight of 10 N on Earth. This is just another way of saying that the gravitational field strength, g, on Earth is 10 N/kg. Remember also, however, that the value of g is different in different parts of the Universe. For example, g on the Moon is only about one-sixth of its value on Earth, approximately 1.6 N/kg.

Examples

1 Find the gravitational potential energy of a mass of 500 grams when raised to a height of 240 cm. Take $g = 10$ N/kg.

Answer

500 grams is 0.5 kg, and 240 cm is 2.4 m.

$$GPE = mgh$$
$$= 0.5 \times 10 \times 2.4$$
$$= \mathbf{12\,J}$$

2 How much heat and sound energy is produced when a mass of 1.2 kg falls to the ground from a height of 5 m? Take $g = 10$ N/kg.

Answer

heat and sound energy produced = original GPE
$$= mgh$$
$$= 1.2 \times 10 \times 5$$
$$= \mathbf{60\,J}$$

3 How much gravitational potential energy is stored in the reservoir of a hydroelectric power station if it holds 5 000 000 kg water at an average height of 80 m above the turbines?

Answer

$$GPE = mgh$$
$$= 5\,000\,000 \times 10 \times 80$$
$$= \mathbf{4\,000\,000\,000\,J} \text{ (or } 4 \times 10^9 \text{ J)}$$

4 A marble of mass 50 g falls to the earth. At the moment of impact its kinetic energy is 1 J. From what height did it fall?

Answer

50 g is 50/1000 = 0.05 kg.

$$GPE = mgh = KE$$
$$= 1\,J$$
$$0.05 \times 10 \times h = 1$$
$$h = \frac{1}{0.05 \times 10}$$
$$= \mathbf{2\,m}$$

GRAVITATIONAL POTENTIAL ENERGY

> **5** A book of mass 500 g has a gravitational potential energy of 3.2 J when at a height of 4 m above the surface of the Moon. Find the gravitational field strength on the Moon.
>
> **Answer**
> 500 g is 500/1000 = 0.5 kg.
> $$GPE = mgh$$
> $$3.2 = 0.5 \times g \times 4$$
> $$g = \frac{3.2}{0.5 \times 4}$$
> $$= 1.6 \, N/kg$$

Questions

17 Competitors in the World's Strongest Man competition must throw a cement block of mass 100 kg over a wall 5.5 m high. How much work is done if the block just clears the top of the wall?

18 A man pushes a lawn mower with a force of 60 N. How much work does he do when he pushes the lawn mower 20 m?

19 The electrical energy used by a boiler is 1000 kJ. The useful output energy is 750 kJ.
  a) Calculate the efficiency of the boiler.
  b) Suggest what might have happened to the energy wasted by the boiler.

20 Explain why the efficiency of a device can never be greater than 1 (or 100%).

21 A car engine has an efficiency of 0.28. How much input chemical energy must be supplied if the total output useful energy is to be 140 000 kJ?

22 The power of the motor in an electric car is 3600 W. How much electrical energy is converted into other energy forms in 5 minutes?

23 A crane can produce a maximum output power of 3000 W. It raises a load of mass 1500 kg through a vertical height of 12 m at a steady speed.
  a) What is the weight of the load?
  b) How much useful work does the crane do lifting the load 12 m?
  c) How long does it take the crane to raise the load 12 m?
  d) At what speed will the load rise through the air?

24 A barrel of weight 1000 N is pushed up a ramp. The barrel rises vertically 40 cm when it is pushed 1 m along the ramp.
  a) Calculate how much useful work is done when the barrel is pushed 1 m along the ramp.
  b) Pushing the barrel 1 m along the ramp requires 1200 J of energy. Calculate the efficiency of the ramp.

Kinetic energy

The **kinetic energy** of an object is the energy it has because it is moving. It can be shown that an object's kinetic energy is given by the formula:

$$KE = \tfrac{1}{2}mv^2$$

where m is its mass in kg and v is its speed in m/s.

Examples

1. A car of mass 800 kg is travelling at 15 m/s. Find its kinetic energy.

Answer

$$KE = \tfrac{1}{2}mv^2$$
$$= \tfrac{1}{2} \times 800 \times 15^2$$
$$= \mathbf{90\,000\,J}$$

2. A bullet has a mass of 20 g and is travelling at 300 m/s. Find its kinetic energy.

Answer

20 g is 20/1000 = 0.02 kg
$$KE = \tfrac{1}{2}mv^2$$
$$= \tfrac{1}{2} \times 0.02 \times 300^2$$
$$= \mathbf{900\,J}$$

3. Find the speed of a boat if its mass is 1200 kg and it has a kinetic energy of 9600 J.

Answer

$$KE = \tfrac{1}{2}mv^2$$
$$9600 = \tfrac{1}{2} \times 1200 \times v^2$$
$$v^2 = \frac{2 \times 9600}{1200}$$
$$= 16$$
$$v = \mathbf{4\,m/s}$$

4. The input power of a small hydroelectric power station is 1 MW. If 18 000 000 kg of water flows past the turbines every hour, find the average speed of the water.

Answer

1 hour = 60 × 60 seconds = 3600 seconds

$$\text{mass of water flowing every second} = \frac{18\,000\,000}{3600}$$
$$= 5000\,kg/s$$

KINETIC ENERGY

> **DID YOU KNOW?**
>
> Niagara Falls is approximately 50 m high and about 5 000 000 kg of water flow over the falls every second. This would give it a maximum capacity to produce 2500 MW of electricity.

Since a 1 MW power station produces 1 000 000 J of electrical energy per second, the minimum kinetic energy of the water passing every second is 1 000 000 J.

$$KE = \tfrac{1}{2} mv^2$$
$$1\,000\,000 = \tfrac{1}{2} \times 5000 \times v^2$$
$$v^2 = \frac{2 \times 1\,000\,000}{5000}$$
$$= 400$$
$$v = 20 \text{ m/s}$$

Questions

25 A communications satellite of mass 120 kg orbits the Earth at a speed of 3000 m/s. Calculate its kinetic energy.

26 The viewing platform at the Eiffel Tower in Paris is about 280 m from the ground. Find the gravitational potential energy of a rubber of mass 50 g on the viewing platform. Compare this to the kinetic energy of a 10 g bullet travelling at 150 m/s fired from a pistol. Comment on your answer.

27 An oil tanker has a mass of 100 000 tonnes. Its kinetic energy is 200 MJ. Calculate its speed.

(1 tonne = 1000 kg; 1 MJ = 1 megajoule = 1 000 000 J)

28 A ball of mass 2 kg falls from rest from a height of 5 m above the ground. Copy the table below and complete it to show the gravitational potential energy, the kinetic energy, the speed and the total energy of the falling ball at different heights above the surface.

Height above ground in m	Gravitational potential energy in J	Kinetic energy in J	Total energy in J	Speed in m/s
5.0		0	100	0
4.0				4.47
	64			
1.8		64		
0.0		0		

29 A car of mass 800 kg is travelling at a steady speed. The kinetic energy of the car is 160 000 J. Show that the speed of the car is 72 km per hour.

30 On planet X, an object of mass 2 kg is raised 10 m above the surface. At that height, the object has a gravitational potential energy of 176 J. Details of three planets are given below. Which one of these three planets is most likely to be planet X?

Planet	Mercury	Venus	Jupiter
Gravitational field strength in N/kg	3.7	8.8	26.4

31 A bouncing ball of mass 200 g leaves the ground with a kinetic energy of 10 J.

  a) If the ball rises vertically, calculate the maximum height it is likely to reach.

  b) In practice, the ball rarely reaches the maximum height. Explain why this is so.

32 The diagram shows energy transfers in a mobile phone.

  a) Use the figures on the diagram to calculate the phone's efficiency.

  b) What principle of physics did you use to calculate the useful sound energy produced?

33 The diagram shows a rotary engine, which has an efficiency of 0.3.

  a) Calculate the amount of useful energy it produces when the input chemical energy is 2000 J.

  b) 90% of the wasted energy is heat. What percentage of the input energy is lost as heat?

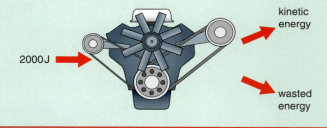

Search
- fossil + fuel
- energy + power
- natural + gas
- coal
- uranium energy + work
- geothermal
- oil
- tidal + energy

Exam questions

1 a) A satellite orbits the Earth.

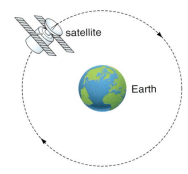

Name the two main types of energy possessed by the satellite in its orbit. *(2 marks)*

b) The diagram below shows a wind farm. This is a site where turbines have been set up.

i) Copy and complete the diagram below to show the useful energy change that takes place in a wind turbine.

Input		Useful output
_____ energy of the wind	→	_____ energy

(2 marks)

ii) The wind is a renewable energy source. What does this mean? *(1 mark)*

iii) Give two other examples of renewable energy resources. *(2 marks)*

c) In Scotland, hydroelectric power makes a significant contribution as a source of electricity.

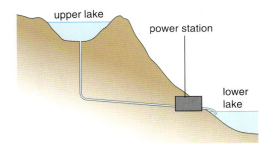

Copy and complete the boxes below to show the energy changes taking place in a hydroelectric power station. *(3 marks)*

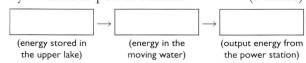

(energy stored in the upper lake) → (energy in the moving water) → (output energy from the power station)

2 A tidal barrage in France generates electricity. One environmental effect of using the tides to generate electricity is to reduce the greenhouse effect by decreasing the consumption of fossil fuels.

Apart from this environmental issue, state one advantage and one disadvantage of generating electricity from the tides. *(2 marks)*

3 a) The most common energy resources used in Europe today are oil, natural gas, coal, nuclear energy, hydroelectric and wind energy.

i) Choose one non-renewable energy resource from the list above and say why it is non-renewable. *(2 marks)*

ii) Choose one renewable energy resource from the list above and say why it is renewable. *(2 marks)*

iii) Give one advantage that non-renewable energy resources have over renewable energy resources. *(1 mark)*

b) It has been estimated that 1×10^8 kg (100 000 000 kg) of water flows over Niagara Falls every second. The falls are 50 metres high.

i) Calculate the gravitational potential energy lost every second by the water flowing over the falls. ($g = 10$ N/kg) *(3 marks)*

A feasibility study has shown that only 0.8% of the available potential energy could be converted into electrical energy by a hydroelectric power station built on the falls.

ii) Calculate the maximum power output of such a hydroelectric power station. *(3 marks)*

iii) Explain why all hydroelectric power stations are dependent on the energy of the Sun. *(2 marks)*

c) The following diagram shows a vehicle with a winch attached. The winch is connected to a tree by a rope. As the winch winds in the rope, the vehicle moves forward towards the tree. The winch uses 500 W of input electrical power. It has an efficiency of 0.6.

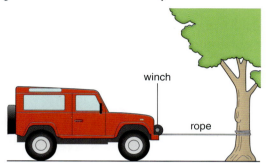

i) Calculate the useful output power of the winch. *(3 marks)*

ii) Write down the useful work done by the winch in 1 second. *(1 mark)*

iii) The pulling force in the rope is 1200 N. Calculate the constant speed at which the vehicle moves forward. *(3 marks)*

4 a) How much work is done by a tractor when it lifts a load of 8000 N to a height of 1.8 m? *(3 marks)*

b) The output power of the tractor is 5.2 kW. How long does it take to do 26 000 J of work? *(3 marks)*

c) The efficiency of the tractor is 0.26 (or 26%). If the output power of the tractor is 5.2 kW, calculate the input power. *(3 marks)*

5 Stephen weighs 550 N. How much work does he do in climbing up to a diving board which is 3.0 m high? *(3 marks)*

6 Saltburn is a seaside resort in Yorkshire. There is a considerable drop from the cliff top to the beach. In 1884, an inclined tramway was built to carry passengers from the beach to the cliff top.

Two identical tramcars were used, each with a water tank underneath it. The tramcars were connected by a steel cable which passed around a large pulley at the top. The tramcar that happens to be at the top has water added until there is enough to raise the tramcar at the bottom of the tramway.

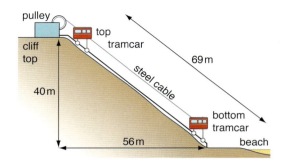

a) On one journey, the weight of the lower tramcar and its passengers was 24 000 N. Ignoring friction, calculate the work done, in kJ, in bringing the tramcar from the beach to the cliff top. *(3 marks)*

b) The time for this journey was 20 seconds. Calculate the power needed to raise the tramcar. *(3 marks)*

c) On this journey, the energy provided by the upper car as it descended was 1200 kJ. Calculate the efficiency of the tramway on this journey. *(3 marks)*

d) During the journey, certain energy changes take place. Copy and complete the table below by writing whether the energy listed in the first column increases, decreases or remains unchanged as the top tramcar descends at a constant speed. *(5 marks)*

Energy	Increases/decreases/unchanged
Potential energy of the top tramcar	
Kinetic energy of the top tramcar	
Kinetic energy of the bottom tramcar	
Potential energy of the bottom tramcar	
Heat energy	

7 A basketball player throws a ball up into the air.

Copy and complete the following table by putting ticks (✓) in the appropriate boxes to show what happens to each quantity *as the ball rises*. Ignore the effects of friction. *(4 marks)*

Quantity	Increases	Decreases	Constant
Speed of ball			
Potential energy of ball			
Total energy of ball			
Kinetic energy of ball			

8 Labels like the one shown below are used in retail to advise customers about the efficiency of domestic appliances.

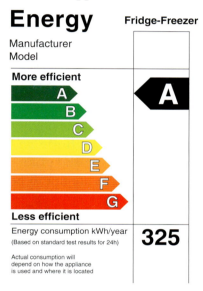

a) Mrs Johnston wants to buy a new dishwasher. She has a choice of a Grade D dishwasher or a Grade A dishwasher.
Which would *cost less* to run? *(1 mark)*

b) Complete the diagram below to describe the main energy changes that take place in a dishwasher. *(4 marks)*

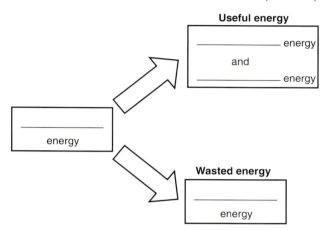

c) Suggest why a shopper might not always buy the most efficient appliance which a shop has for sale. *(2 marks)*

Radioactivity

▶ Atomic structure and radioactivity

The structure of atoms

We take it for granted today that all matter is made up of **atoms** – but what are atoms made of? Experiments carried out by J.J. Thomson and Lord Rutherford led physicists in the early part of the twentieth century to believe that atoms themselves had a structure.

Evidence for the existence of electrons

When a current goes through a metal wire, the wire gets hot. If the wire is hot enough, it emits negatively charged particles. If the wire itself is connected to the negative terminal of a battery, these negatively charged particles are repelled from the wire, called the **cathode**, and can be collected by a positive plate, the **anode**. The wire and plate must be in a vacuum if the negatively charged particles are not to be deflected by collisions with gas atoms.

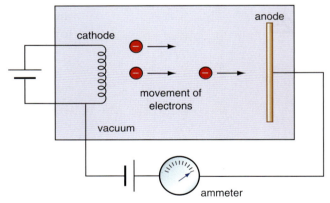

Figure 1 Demonstrating the existence of electrons

The process is called **thermionic emission**. Early in the twentieth century, physicists were able to show that these particles came from the atoms of the metal filament. Thomson called them **electrons**. Their attraction to the positive plate showed clearly that they were negatively charged.

Since these electrons were so easily deflected by a magnet, Thomson knew that they were very, very light compared to the atoms that emitted them. He also realised that because atoms themselves are electrically neutral, there had to be some part of the atom that had a positive charge.

How were the electrons arranged in atoms? One of the earliest models was the '**plum-pudding**' or '**currant-bun**' model in which electrons were dotted throughout the atom like currants in a bun. The positive charge was thought to spread throughout the volume like the dough of the bun.

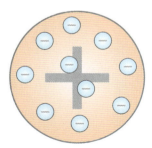

Figure 2 The 'plum-pudding' model of the atom

> **DID YOU KNOW?**
>
> The name 'electron' was suggested by Irish physicist George Johnstone Stoney in 1894, but credit for the discovery of the particle itself goes to the Englishman J.J. Thomson.

58

ATOMIC STRUCTURE AND RADIOACTIVITY

Evidence for the existence of nuclei

Partly to test Thomson's theory, Rutherford suggested that the recently discovered positively charged alpha particles (see later) might be fired at a thin gold foil. Most of the alpha particles went straight through the foil with little or no deflection. But what really shocked the Rutherford team was that some alpha particles were deflected through very large angles – and a few even came straight back at them. Rutherford then realised that there had to be something 'hard' inside the atom to cause this strange 'back scattering' – he called it the atomic **nucleus**.

Rutherford argued that because most of the alpha particles missed the nucleus, it had to be very small. Since it appeared to repel the positively charged alpha particles, the nucleus had to be positively charged. But why did most of the alpha particles pass straight through the atom? Rutherford correctly argued that most of the atom was really just empty space.

Finally, Rutherford realised that because the electron was so light, most of the atom's mass was contained within the nucleus itself.

Later, in order to explain how certain elements gave out light, Rutherford suggested that the electrons orbited the nucleus in circular paths. So the plum-pudding model gave way to the planetary model, with the orbiting electrons pictured like planets orbiting the Sun.

Rutherford's gold foil experiment took place around 1909–10. It was not until 1933 that convincing evidence was presented by James Chadwick that there were two different types of particle in the nucleus – uncharged neutrons as well as positively charged protons.

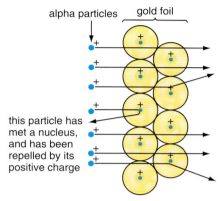

Figure 3 Most of the alpha particles pass straight through the gold foil or are slightly deflected – a very few make a 'direct hit' on the nucleus and bounce back

⇨ DID YOU KNOW?

The nucleus of almost every atom contains protons and neutrons. At one time it was thought that protons and neutrons had no structure, but we now know that both are made of mysterious particles called quarks.

The planetary model of the atom

The relative masses and charges of the particles that make up the atom are given in Table 1.

Particle	Location	Relative mass*	Relative charge*
Proton	Within the nucleus	1	+1
Neutron	Within the nucleus	1	0
Electron	Orbiting the nucleus	$\frac{1}{1840}$	−1

*Mass and charge are measured relative to the proton

Table 1

A neutral atom must have the same number of protons as orbiting electrons. Figure 4 shows a helium atom. There are two orbiting electrons, so there must also be two protons in the nucleus. Note that the diagram is not to scale – the diameter of the atom (about 1×10^{-10} m) is about 100 000 times greater than that of the nucleus (about 1×10^{-15} m).

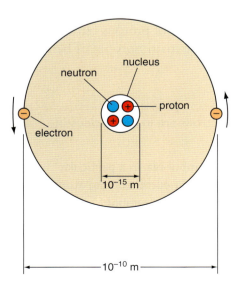

Figure 4 A helium atom

RADIOACTIVITY

Atomic number and mass number

The number of protons in the nucleus of an atom determines what the atom is. All hydrogen nuclei have one proton, all helium nuclei have two protons, all lithium nuclei have three protons and so on. The number of protons is called the **atomic number** and is given the symbol Z.

As the mass of the electrons is negligible, the total number of particles in the nucleus determines the total mass of an atom. Particles in the nucleus are called nucleons, so the **mass number** (or nucleon number) is the sum of the number of protons and the number of neutrons. Mass number is given the symbol A.

Every nucleus can therefore be written in the form $^{A}_{Z}X$, where X is the chemical symbol, A is the mass number and Z is the atomic number.

For example, uranium is given the chemical symbol U. All uranium nuclei have 92 protons in the nucleus. One form of uranium, called uranium-235, has a mass number of 235. This means it has 92 protons and 143 neutrons ($235 - 92 = 143$). A uranium nucleus is given the symbol $^{235}_{92}U$. It is important to realise that this is the symbol for the **nucleus** of the atom – orbiting electrons are ignored.

You will notice that the top number gives the mass of the nucleus, and that the bottom number gives the positive charge. This same system can also be used to describe protons, neutrons and electrons.

> proton, $^{1}_{1}p$ neutron, $^{1}_{0}n$ electron, $^{0}_{-1}e$

> Atomic number,
> Z = number of protons
> Mass number,
> A = number of protons
>   + number of neutrons
>   = number of nucleons

Isotopes

Not all the atoms of the same element have the same mass. For example, one form of helium (helium-3) has three nucleons and another form (helium-4) has four nucleons. But all helium nuclei have two protons. So, helium-3 has two protons and one neutron; helium-4 has two protons and two neutrons (Figure 5).

Physicists call atoms with the same number of protons but a different number of neutrons **isotopes**. The main isotopes of helium are $^{3}_{2}He$ and $^{4}_{2}He$.

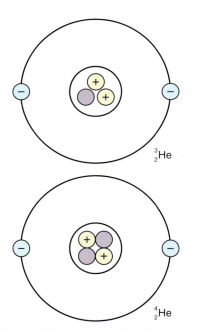

Figure 5 The structure of helium-3 and helium-4

DID YOU KNOW?

The only Irishman to have won a Nobel Prize for Physics was E.T.S. Walton. His award was for building and using one of the earliest accelerators – or 'atom-smashers'. Until recently, his daughter was teaching physics in Belfast.

Questions

1. How many protons, neutrons and electrons are in the nucleus of carbon-14 if its symbol is $^{14}_{6}C$?

2. The element sodium has the chemical symbol Na. In a particular sodium isotope, there are 12 neutrons. In a neutral sodium atom there are 11 orbiting electrons. Write down the symbol for the nucleus of this isotope.

3. In what way are the nuclei of isotopes the same? In what way are they different?

Radiation

In 1896, the French scientist Henri Becquerel discovered that certain rocks containing uranium give out strange radiation that could penetrate paper and fog photographic film. He called the effect **radioactivity**. His students, Pierre and Marie Curie, were later to identify three separate types of radiation. Unsure of a suitable name, the Curies called them alpha (α), beta (β) and gamma (γ) radiation after the first three letters of the Greek alphabet. For their work on radioactivity, the Curies and Henri Becquerel were jointly awarded the Nobel Prize for Physics in 1903.

It is important to realise that the disintegration of nuclei in radioactivity is both **random** and **spontaneous**. This means that we cannot influence when a particular nucleus will disintegrate. The process is not related to chemistry – so heating the source or grinding it to a fine powder will have no effect on the rate of decay. Nor can a catalyst ever be found to speed up or slow down the rate of radioactive decay.

Radioactive material is found naturally all around us and inside our bodies. A small minority of carbon atoms are radioactive carbon-14 isotopes. They are found in the carbon dioxide in the air and in the cells of all living organisms. Traces of radioactive elements, for example potassium, can be found in our food. Certain rocks contain uranium, all the isotopes of which are radioactive, and this decays giving radon, a radioactive gas. There is also radiation reaching Earth from outer space. All these natural sources are known together as **background radiation**.

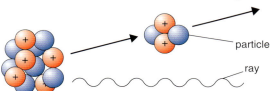

Figure 6 An unstable nucleus emitting a particle and a ray

Ionising radiation

The nuclei of some atoms are unstable and emit radiation. This is known as ionising radiation because as it passes through matter it causes some of the atoms to become ions.

Types of radiation

Alpha (α) radiation

* Alpha radiation is made up of a stream of separate alpha particles emitted from large nuclei.
* An alpha particle is a helium nucleus with two protons and two neutrons – so it has a relative atomic mass of 4.
* Alpha particles are positively charged and so will be deflected in a magnetic field.
* Alpha particles have poor powers of penetration and can travel through only a few centimetres of air. They can easily be stopped by a sheet of paper.
* Alpha radiation has the strongest ionising power.

Beta (β) radiation

* Beta radiation is made up of a stream of beta particles emitted from nuclei in which the number of neutrons is much larger than the number of protons.
* A beta particle is a fast-moving electron, which is formed in the nucleus – so it has relative atomic mass of about $\frac{1}{1840}$.
* Beta particles are negatively charged, so they will be deflected in a magnetic field. This deflection will be greater than that of alpha particles because beta particles have much smaller mass.
* Beta particles move much faster than alpha particles and so have a greater penetrating power.
* Beta particles can travel several metres in air, but are stopped by 5 mm thick aluminium foil.
* Beta radiation has an ionising power between that of alpha and gamma radiation.

Gamma (γ) radiation

* Unlike the other types of radiation, gamma radiation does not consist of particles but of high-energy waves.
* Like alpha and beta radiation, gamma radiation comes from a disintegrating unstable nucleus.
* Because it is not a particle, gamma radiation has no mass.
* Because there are no charged particles, a magnetic field has no effect on gamma radiation.
* Gamma radiation has great penetrating power, travelling a very large range in air.
* A thick block of lead or concrete is used to greatly reduce the effects of gamma radiation, but is not able to stop it completely.
* Gamma radiation has the weakest ionising power.

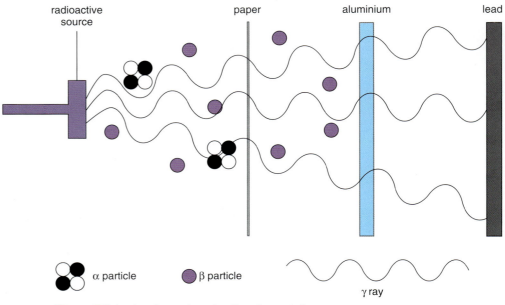

Figure 7 Selective absorption of radioactive emissions

Uses of radiation

* Carbon dating of organic material. All living organisms contain some carbon-14. When the organism is alive, the ratio of carbon-12 atoms to carbon-14 atoms remains constant. After the organism dies, the amount of carbon-14 decreases as the radioactive isotope decays. Comparing the amount of carbon-14 present in a sample with the amount in a living organism allows calculation of the age of the sample. Fortunately carbon-14 has a long half-life (see later) and so decays slowly. This method was used to date the Dead Sea Scrolls.
* Gamma radiation from the cobalt-60 isotope can be used to treat tumours (Figure 8).
* Gamma radiation can be used to treat fresh food. By killing bacteria on the food, this helps to keep the food fresh for longer. The use is controversial, however – many people are worried about the long-term effects on the human body of eating irradiated food. Ideally the radioisotope used should have a very long half-life so that it is a long time before it needs to be replaced.
* Surgical instruments and hospital dressings can be sterilised by exposure to gamma radiation (Figure 9). Again, the source should have a very long half-life.
* Beta radiation can be used to monitor the thickness of sheets of paper or aluminium. An emitter is placed on one side of the sheet and a detector on the other. As the sheet moves past, the activity detected will be the same, so long as the thickness remains unchanged. If there is a change in thickness, the equipment can trigger the rollers to squeeze harder or less to maintain the thickness within an acceptable range.

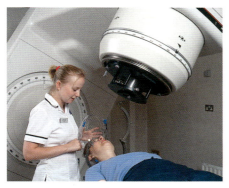

Figure 8 Radiotherapy involves the use of radioactive materials to treat cancers

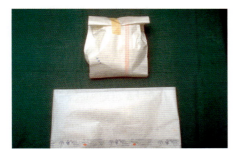

Figure 9 Operating equipment is sterilised by gamma rays

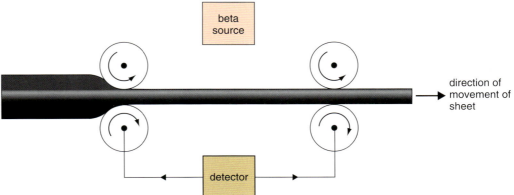

Figure 10 Using a long half-life beta source to control the thickness of an aluminium sheet

* A suitable radioactive isotope can be used to provide information about fluid movement to monitor, for example, leaks in underground pipes. The radiation needs to penetrate many centimetres of soil to reach the detectors – this means that the source must be a gamma emitter. Only gamma rays have sufficient penetrating power. But to avoid dangerous radioactive materials being in the ground for a long time the source should have a short half-life.

RADIOACTIVITY

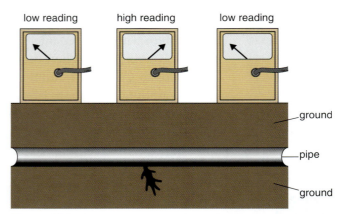

Figure 11 Radioactive tracers can be used to locate a leak in a pipe

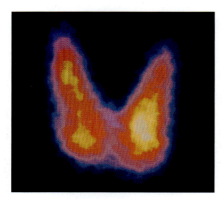

Figure 12 This scan shows radioactive iodine-131 localised in the thyroid gland

* Iodine-131 is used in investigations of the thyroid gland.

Great care must be taken when using radioactive isotopes because radiation can damage living cells by altering the structure of a cell's chemicals. Protective clothing must be worn and the amount of time that the worker is exposed to the radiation must be strictly controlled. Radioactive isotopes that are taken internally are usually not alpha emitters, because they are such powerful ionisers, and they must have a short half-life so that they do not remain in the tissues for too long.

Nuclear equations

Symbol equations can be written to represent alpha and beta decay. The alpha particle can be written as $^{4}_{2}\alpha$ or $^{4}_{2}He$ and the beta particle as $^{0}_{-1}\beta$ or $^{0}_{-1}e$.

For example:

* Alpha decay of uranium-238

   $^{238}_{92}U \rightarrow {}^{234}_{90}Th + {}^{4}_{2}He$ (or α)

* Beta decay of carbon-14

   $^{14}_{6}C \rightarrow {}^{14}_{7}N + {}^{0}_{-1}e$ (or β)

When writing symbol equations it is important to remember that:

* the total mass number on the left-hand side must equal the total mass number on the right-hand side
* the total atomic numbers must be the same on both sides.

If you know the original isotope and the one formed by the decay, it is possible to determine the type of decay by working out the type of particle emitted.

If you know the original isotope and the type of decay, you can work out the isotope that is formed by the decay.

Example

Radium-226 decays to polonium-222. Radium (Ra) has atomic number 86 and polonium (Po) has atomic number 84.
Which type of decay occurs?

RADIATION

Answer

$$^{226}_{86}Ra \rightarrow \ ^{222}_{84}Po + \ ^{A}_{Z}X$$

mass number: $226 = 222 + A$

$$A = 4$$

atomic number: $86 = 84 + Z$

$$Z = 2$$

The particle with a mass number of 4 and an atomic number of 2 is helium – so X is an alpha particle and the type of decay is alpha.

Questions

4 Work out the type of decay in each of the following examples:
  a) bismuth-213 to polonium-213
  b) radium-226 to radon-222
  c) francium-221 to actinium-217.

5 Work out the name and mass number of the isotope formed in each of the following examples:
  a) alpha decay of polonium-214
  b) beta decay of lead-212
  c) beta decay of thallium-210.

6 a) How does the value of the mass number change in alpha decay?
  b) How does the value of the atomic number change in alpha decay?
  c) How does the value of the mass number change in beta decay?
  d) How does the value of the atomic number change in beta decay?

> The **half-life** of an isotope is defined as the time taken for its radioactivity to fall by half.

Half-life

As a sample of a radioactive isotope decays, the activity of the sample decreases.

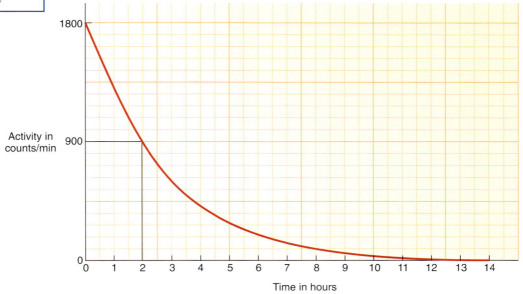

Figure 13 The radioactive decay curve for a substance with a half-life of 2 hours

RADIOACTIVITY

All the different isotopes have specific and constant half-lives. Some half-lives are very short — a matter of seconds or even a fraction of a second — and others can be thousands of years. Table 2 gives the half-lives of some common radioactive isotopes.

Isotope	Half-life
Uranium-238	4 500 000 000 years
Carbon-14	5730 years
Phosphorus-30	2.5 minutes
Oxygen-15	2.06 minutes
Barium-144	11.4 seconds
Polonium-216	0.145 seconds

Table 2

The unit of radioactivity

Radioactivity can only be detected when unstable nuclei decay. The greater the number of disintegrations taking place every second, the greater is the radioactivity. The unit for radioactivity is the Becquerel (Bq); 1 Bq = 1 disintegration per second.

Examples of half-life calculations

1. What mass of nitrogen-13 would remain if 80 g decayed for 30 minutes? Nitrogen-13 has a half-life of 10 minutes.

Answer

Mass of nitrogen-13 remaining	Time in half-lives	Time in minutes
80 g	0	0
40 g	1	10
20 g	2	20
10 g	3	30

10 g would remain after **30 minutes**.

2. How long would it take for 20 g of cobalt-60 to decay to 5 g? The half-life of cobalt-60 is 5.26 years.

Answer

20 g to 10 g takes 5.26 years; and 10 g to 5 g takes another 5.26 years. Total time taken is **10.52 years**.

3. Strontium-93 takes 32 minutes to decay to 6.25% of its original mass. Calculate the value of its half-life.

Answer

% of strontium-93 remaining	Time in half-lives	Time in minutes
100	0	
50	1	
25	2	
12.5	3	
6.25	4	32

From the table, 4 half-lives take 32 minutes.

Each half-life = $\frac{32}{4}$ minutes = 8 minutes.

The half-life of strontium-93 is **8 minutes**.

4 When a radioactive material with a half-life of 24 hours arrives in a hospital, its activity is 1000 Bq. Calculate its activity 24 hours before, and also 72 hours after its arrival.

Answer

Activity in Bq	Time in half-lives	Time in hours
2000	−1	−24
1000 (arrives)	0	0
500	1	24
250	2	48
125	3	72

Activity 24 hours before arrival is **2000 Bq**.

Activity 72 hours after arrival is **125 Bq**.

5 Plot a graph of activity (y-axis) against time (x-axis) using the data in Question 4. Start the graph from time = 0 and activity = 1000 Bq. Use the graph to find the activity 36 hours after the material arrives at the hospital.

Answer

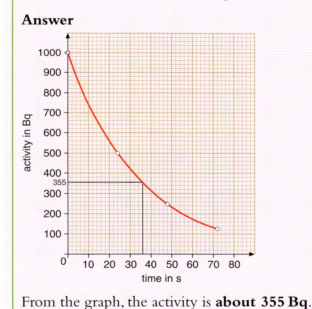

From the graph, the activity is **about 355 Bq**.

Practical work with radioactive materials

Students under the age of 16 are expressly forbidden to handle radioactive sources.

The most common type of radiation detector is the Geiger-Müller tube (GM tube) connected to a counter or a ratemeter.

When alpha, beta or gamma radiation enters the GM tube, it causes some of the argon gas inside to ionise and give an electrical discharge. This discharge is detected and counted by the counter. If the counter is connected to its internal speaker, you can hear the click when radiation enters the tube.

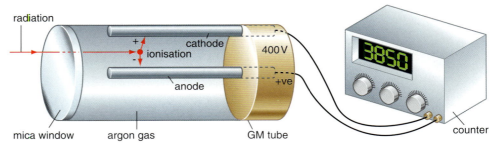

Figure 14 Section through a GM tube

You don't have to know how a GM tube works, but it is important to know how it could be used to do practical work on radiation.

Measuring the background radiation

First remove known sources of radiation from the laboratory. Then set the GM counter to zero. Switch on the counter and start a stopwatch. After 30 minutes, read the count on the counter. Divide the count by 30 to obtain the background count rate in counts per minute. A typical figure is around 15 counts per minute. Fortunately, the background count in Northern Ireland does not present a serious health risk.

The background count must always be subtracted from any other count when measuring the activity from a specific source.

Precautions when using closed radioactive sources in schools

* Always store the sources in a lead-lined box, under lock and key, when not required for experimental use.
* Always handle sources using tongs, holding the source at arm's length and pointing it away from any bystander.
* Always work with sources quickly and methodically to minimise the dose to the user.

Measuring the approximate range of radiation

Alpha

* Place a GM tube on a wooden cradle and connect it to a ratemeter.
* Hold an alpha source directly in front of the window of the tube, and slowly increase the distance between the source and the tube. At about 3 cm (depending on the source used) the ratemeter reading falls dramatically to that of background radiation.
* Fix a thin piece of paper in contact with the window of the GM tube. Bring the alpha source up to the paper so that the casing of the source touches it. The reading on the ratemeter is no greater than the background count, showing that the alpha particles can't penetrate the paper.

Beta

* Fix a 1 mm thick piece of aluminium in contact with the window of the GM tube.
* Bring a beta source up to the aluminium so that the casing of the source touches it.

RADIATION

* The reading on the ratemeter is observed to be significantly above the background count, showing that some beta particles have penetrated the aluminium.
* Repeat the process with 2 mm, 3 mm etc. thick pieces of aluminium. At about 5 mm there is a significant reduction in the count rate on the ratemeter, indicating the approximate range of beta particles in aluminium.

Gamma

If the beta particle experiment is repeated with a gamma source, there is practically no reduction in the count rate for a 5 mm thick piece of aluminium. If the aluminium sheets are replaced by lead, it will be found that even school sources will give gamma radiation that can easily penetrate several centimetres of lead.

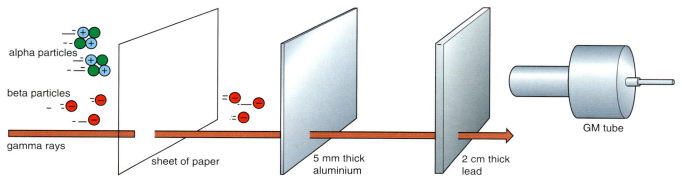

Figure 15 The penetrative range of the three types of radiation

> **DID YOU KNOW?**
>
> Some waste materials from nuclear power stations will remain radioactive for tens of thousands of years. The best way to deal with the storage of these materials remains a challenge for physicists and engineers.

Nuclear fission and nuclear fusion

Nuclear fission

Radioactivity involves the random disintegration of unstable nuclei. But some heavy nuclei, like those of uranium, can actually be forced to split into two lighter nuclei. The process is called **nuclear fission**. This usually comes about as a result of the heavy nucleus being struck by a slow neutron. The heavy nucleus splits and the fragments move apart at very high speed, carrying with them a vast amount of energy. At the same time, two or three fast neutrons are also emitted – these are the fission neutrons. The fission neutrons go on to produce further fission and so create a chain reaction.

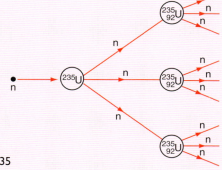

Figure 16a The fission of a uranium-235 nucleus

Figure 16b A chain reaction in uranium-235

69

Just how much energy is emitted in fission? The fission of a single uranium nucleus produces about 40 000 000 times more energy than would be produced by a single carbon atom (in coal) reacting with oxygen to produce carbon dioxide. It did not take long for physicists to realise the huge potential of energy production using nuclear fission.

In a nuclear power station, steps are taken to ensure that, on average, just one of the fission neutrons goes on to produce further fission – this is controlled nuclear fission. The heat produced in the reaction is used to turn water into steam, which drives turbines to generate electricity. In a nuclear bomb, there is no attempt to control the fission process – the energy is released devastatingly quickly.

A major disadvantage of all fission processes is that the fission fragments are almost always highly radioactive. This type of radioactive waste is extremely dangerous, and expensive measures must be taken to store it until the level of activity is sufficiently small. In some cases, this means that the waste must be stored deep underground in a vitrified (glass-like) state for tens of thousands of years. The danger is that over time, the containers may leak and cause underground water pollution. A further danger comes from earthquakes – these can rupture containers of radioactive waste buried underground, causing the radioactive material to leak into the soil and to contaminate water sources.

Even in Britain, there are over 200 earthquakes every year, many so weak that they are barely recorded. But as recently as February 2008, there was an earthquake of magnitude 5.2 in Lincolnshire. This lasted for roughly 10 seconds and caused some structural damage. The tremors were felt across a wide area of England and Wales, and as far west as Bangor, Northern Ireland.

Nuclear fusion

This is the process which goes on in stars like our Sun. At the centre of the Sun the temperature is about 15 000 000°C. At this temperature, the nuclei of atoms are stripped of their orbiting electrons and they are moving at a tremendously high speed. Being positively charged, the nuclei would normally repel each other, but if they are moving fast enough they can join (or **fuse**) to form a new nucleus.

In the Sun, hydrogen isotopes known as deuterium (hydrogen-2) and tritium (hydrogen-3) collide and fuse to create a new nucleus, helium-4. This causes the release of a vast amount of energy, some of which eventually reaches Earth as electromagnetic radiation. The equation representing this process is:

$$^{2}_{1}H + ^{3}_{1}H \rightarrow ^{4}_{2}He + ^{1}_{0}n + \text{energy}$$

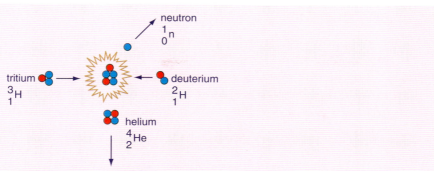

Figure 17 The fusion of deuterium and tritium

There have been many attempts to obtain controlled nuclear fusion on Earth – one research centre is at Culham in Oxfordshire. But so far, physicists have faced major difficulties. One is the problem of how to contain the reacting plasma at a high enough temperature and for a sufficiently long time for the reaction to take place. If we learn how to control nuclear fusion here on Earth then the rewards will be enormous. We will have an almost unlimited source of energy (from the hydrogen in water) with harmless waste products (inert helium nuclei).

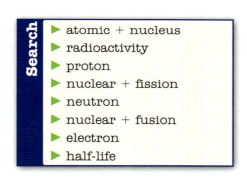

RADIOACTIVITY

Exam questions

1 a) The table shows the particles that make up a neutral carbon atom. Copy and complete the table showing the mass, charge, number and location of the particles. Some information has already been put in the table. *(7 marks)*

Particle	Mass	Charge	Number	Location
Electron		−1		
Neutron	1		6	In the nucleus
Proton			6	

b) Radon is a naturally-occurring radioactive gas.
  i) Explain what is meant by 'radioactive'. *(2 marks)*
  ii) Explain the danger of breathing radon gas into the lungs. *(2 marks)*
  iii) Explain, in terms of the particles that make up the nucleus, the meaning of 'isotope'. *(2 marks)*

c) A student investigated the decay of a radioactive substance. She measured the corrected count rate of the substance every 20 minutes. The half-life of the substance is 20 minutes. At the start, the count rate was 800 counts per minute.
  i) Copy the graph below and plot this point and four more points that she should have found. *(5 marks)*

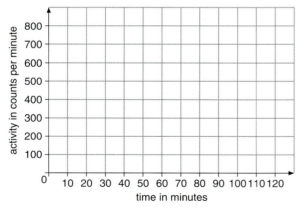

  ii) Draw a smooth curve through the plotted points. *(1 mark)*

d) i) The range of beta radiation in aluminium is several millimetres. Explain what this statement means. *(1 mark)*
  ii) Draw a neat, labelled diagram of the assembled apparatus that could be used to measure the range of beta particles in aluminium. *(3 marks)*
  iii) What measurements would be taken during this experiment? *(3 marks)*
  iv) How would you use these measurements to find the range of beta particles in aluminium? *(2 marks)*
  v) Sketch the graph that you would expect to obtain from these measurements, and mark on it the range of the beta radiation. Label each axis. *(2 marks)*

2 a) The isotope $^{14}_{6}C$ changes into an isotope of nitrogen when it emits a beta particle. The chemical symbol for nitrogen is N. Write down an equation involving atomic numbers and mass numbers to describe this reaction. *(4 marks)*

b) A radioactive isotope of gold emits gamma rays. It is injected into a patient's bloodstream and used to study the working of the patient's heart. The gamma radiation emitted by the gold is detected outside the patient's body by a device called a gamma camera.
Why would a radioactive isotope that emits alpha radiation be unsuitable for this purpose? *(2 marks)*

c) To check the half-life of this isotope of gold, a radiographer measured the activity of a sample of the isotope every 10 s. He then corrected for the background activity. His measurements are shown in the table below.

Corrected activity in counts per second	400	320	250	198	160	100	80
Time in seconds	0	10	20	30	40	60	70

  i) What causes background activity, and how did the radiographer correct his measurements? *(2 marks)*
  ii) Using the measurements above, plot a graph of corrected activity (y-axis) against time (x-axis). *(5 marks)*
  iii) Use the graph to find the half-life of gold. Show clearly how you use the graph to obtain the best value of this half-life. *(2 marks)*

72

3 A radioactive decay series can be represented on a graph of mass number, A, against atomic number, Z. Part of a table for such a series is given below:

Element (symbol)	Atomic number	Mass number	Decays by emitting	Leaving element
U	92	238	α	Th
Th	90	234	β	Pa
Pa	91	234	β	
	92	234	α	
	90	230		Ra
Ra	88	226		Rn
Rn	86			Po
Po		218	α	Pb
Pb				Bi
Bi	83			Po

a) In what ways do mass number and atomic number change in **i)** α decay and **ii)** β decay? *(4 marks)*

b) Copy and complete the table above. *(3 marks)*

c) Plot the points on a graph of mass number (y-axis) against atomic number (x-axis) to show the decay of each element. Join the points with arrows to show the decay. *(5 marks)*

d) Explain why the emission of gamma radiation cannot be shown on such a graph. *(1 mark)*

e) Identify two pairs of isotopes using the table above. *(2 marks)*

4 A sample containing 100 grams of a uranium isotope arrives at a factory. The table below shows how the mass of the isotope changes over time.

Mass of isotope in grams	Time in days
100	0
72	10
52	20
37	30
27	40

a) Explain the meaning of:
   i) half-life   **ii)** isotope. *(2 marks)*

b) Plot a graph of mass of isotope (y-axis) against time (x-axis). *(4 marks)*

c) From the graph, calculate the half-life of this isotope as accurately as possible. *(2 marks)*

d) Estimate the mass of the uranium present in the sample 3 weeks *before* it arrived in the factory. *(2 marks)*

5 A certain material has a half-life of 12 minutes. What proportion of that material would you expect still to be present 1 hour later? *(3 marks)*

6 A detector of radiation is placed close to a radioactive source that has a very long half-life.

In four consecutive 10-second intervals, the following numbers of counts were recorded: 100, 107, 99, 102. Why were the four counts different? *(2 marks)*

5 Waves, sound and light

▶ Types of waves

Waves transfer energy from one point to another but they do not, in general, transfer matter. Radio waves, for example, carry energy from a radio transmitter to your home, but no matter moves in the air as a result.

All waves are produced as a result of **vibrations** and can be classified as **longitudinal** or **transverse**. A vibration is a repeated movement, first in one direction and then in the opposite direction.

Longitudinal waves

A longitudinal wave is one in which the particles vibrate *parallel* to the direction in which the wave is travelling. The only types of longitudinal waves relevant to your GCSE course are:

* sound waves
* ultrasound waves
* slinky spring waves
* P-type earthquake waves.

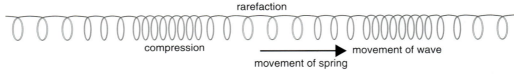

Figure 1 A longitudinal wave moving along a slinky spring

It is easy to demonstrate longitudinal waves by holding a slinky spring at one end and moving your hand backwards and forwards parallel to the axis of the stretched spring. **Compressions** are places where the coils (or particles) bunch together. **Rarefactions** are places where the coils (or particles) are furthest apart.

All longitudinal waves are made up of compressions and rarefactions. In the case of sound waves, the particles are the molecules of the material through which the sound is travelling. These molecules bunch together and separate just as they do in a longitudinal wave on a slinky spring.

Transverse waves

A transverse wave is one in which the vibrations are at 90° to the direction in which the wave is travelling. Most waves in nature are transverse – some examples are:

* water waves
* slinky spring waves
* waves on strings and ropes
* electromagnetic waves.

DESCRIBING WAVES

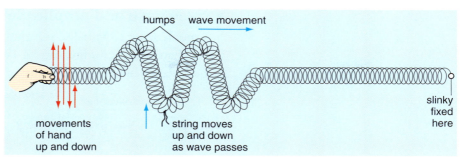

Figure 2 A transverse wave moving along a slinky spring

A transverse wave pulse can be created by shaking one end of a rope. The pulse moves along the rope, but the final position of the rope is exactly the same as it was at the beginning. None of the material of the rope has moved permanently. But the wave pulse has carried energy from one point to another.

Water waves are clearly transverse. A cork floating on the surface of some water bobs up and down as the waves pass. The vertical vibration of the cork is perpendicular to the horizontal motion of the wave. Energy is transferred in the directions in which the wave is travelling.

There are many other examples showing that waves carry energy:

* visible light, infrared radiation and microwaves all make things heat up
* X-rays and gamma waves can damage cells by disrupting DNA
* loud sound waves can cause objects to vibrate (even if that is only your eardrum)
* water waves can be used to generate electricity.

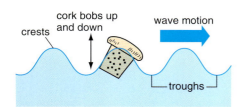

Figure 3 Ripples on water are transverse waves

▶ Describing waves

There are a number of important definitions relating to waves that must be learned.

* The frequency of a wave is the *number of complete waves passing a fixed point in a second*. Frequency is given the symbol f, and is measured in units called **hertz** (abbreviation Hz).
* The **wavelength** of a wave is the *distance between two consecutive crests or troughs*. Wavelength is given the symbol λ, and is measured in metres. λ is the Greek letter 'l' and is pronounced 'lamda'.
* The **amplitude** of a wave is the *greatest displacement of the wave from its undisturbed position*. Amplitude is measured in metres.

> **DID YOU KNOW?**
>
> The sea wave with the largest amplitude was measured in the Pacific Ocean in the 1990s at over 35 metres. Tsunami, often wrongly called tidal waves, can have amplitudes greater than 70 metres.

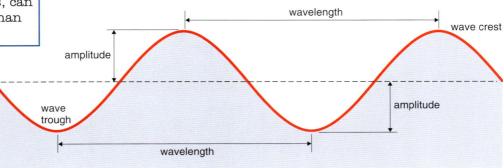

Figure 4 A transverse wave in water showing the wavelength and amplitude

WAVES, SOUND AND LIGHT

Wavelength and amplitude of longitudinal waves

It is much easier to visualise wavelength and amplitude for transverse waves than for longitudinal waves. For a longitudinal wave, the wavelength is the distance between the centre of one compression and the next.

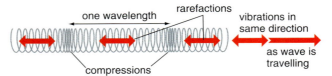

Figure 5 In longitudinal waves, the vibrations are along the same direction as the wave is travelling

But what is the amplitude of a longitudinal wave? Remember that the particles in a longitudinal wave vibrate backwards and forwards parallel to the direction in which the wave is moving. The amplitude of a longitudinal wave is the maximum distance a particle moves from the centre of this motion.

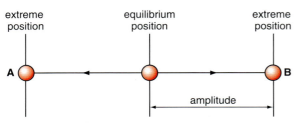

Figure 6 Determining the amplitude of a longitudinal wave

The wave equation

Imagine a wave with wavelength λ (metres) and frequency f (hertz).

From the definition of frequency, f waves pass a fixed point in 1 second.

But each wave has a length λ. So, the total distance travelled every second is $f \times \lambda$.

But the distance travelled in a second is the speed. So:

$$\text{wave speed} = \text{frequency} \times \text{wavelength}$$
or
$$v = f \times \lambda$$

This important equation must be learned for the GCSE examination. Note that the units used in the wave equation must be consistent, as shown in Table 1.

Frequency	Wavelength	Speed
	cm	cm/s
Always in hertz	m	m/s
	km	km/s

Table 1

Examples

1. What is the speed of a water wave of frequency 4 Hz and wavelength 3 cm?

   Answer
   $$v = f \times \lambda$$
   $$= 4 \times 3$$
   $$= 12 \text{ cm/s}$$

2 What is the wavelength of a sound wave of frequency 264 Hz and speed 330 m/s?

Answer

$$v = f \times \lambda$$
$$330 = 264 \times \lambda$$
$$\lambda = \frac{330}{264}$$
$$= 1.25 \text{ m}$$

3 Find the frequency of radio waves of wavelength 1500 m if their speed is 300 Mm/s.

Answer

First note that 300 Mm/s = 300 million metres per second = 300 000 000 m/s. Then apply the wave equation:

$$v = f \times \lambda$$
$$300\,000\,000 = f \times 1500$$
$$f = \frac{300\,000\,000}{1500}$$
$$= 200\,000 \text{ Hz}$$

4 The vertical distance between a crest and a trough is 24 cm and the horizontal distance between the first and fifth wave crests is 40 cm. If 30 such waves pass a fixed point every minute, find the amplitude, frequency, wavelength and speed of these waves.

Answer

$$amplitude = \tfrac{1}{2} \times \text{distance between crest and trough}$$
$$= \tfrac{1}{2} \times 24$$
$$= 12 \text{ cm}$$

$$frequency = \text{no. of waves passing in 1 s}$$
$$= \frac{30 \text{ waves}}{60 \text{ seconds}}$$
$$= 0.5 \text{ Hz}$$

Between the first and fifth wave crests, there are four complete waves so:

$$wavelength = \text{distance between consecutive crests}$$
$$= \tfrac{1}{4} \times 40$$
$$= 10 \text{ cm}$$

$$speed = frequency \times wavelength$$
$$= 0.5 \times 10$$
$$= 5 \text{ cm/s}$$

Questions

1. A stretched slinky spring rests on a table. Waves can be set up on the slinky spring so that the wave profile (shape) will travel from end A to end B.

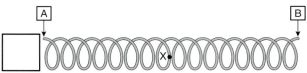

   a) Copy the diagram. In the box at end A, draw an arrow to show the direction of energy flow due to the wave.
   b) Describe how point X will move when a *longitudinal* wave passes along the slinky.
   c) Describe the motion of the particles in a *transverse* wave.
   d) Give an example of a transverse wave, other than those generated on a slinky spring.

2. Sarah generates some water waves in a ripple tank.

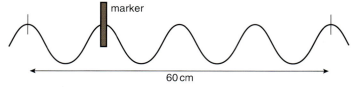

   a) What is the wavelength of the water waves?
   Sarah observes ten waves passing the marker in 4 seconds.
   b) How many waves pass the marker in 1 second?
   c) Use your answer to part b) to state the frequency of the water waves.
   d) Calculate the speed of the water waves.

Plane wave fronts

We can learn much about the behaviour of waves using a ripple tank as shown in Figure 7.

A motor makes a straight dipper vibrate up and down continuously. This produces straight water waves – or **plane waves**. By shining a light from above the tank, we can see bright and dark patches on the screen below. These patches show the wave crests and troughs. The direction of movement of the water waves is always at right angles to the wave fronts.

Water waves move quite quickly and it can sometimes be hard to see what is happening. Looking through a rotating stroboscope can make the waves appear to stand still.

Suppose the stroboscope had 12 slits and rotated twice every second. Then the tank would be seen 24 times a second. If the waves had a frequency of 24 Hz, then every 1/24th of a second, each wave would have moved forward by *exactly* one wavelength. So the wave pattern when viewed through the stroboscope would appear to be *stationary*.

Figure 7 Viewing the wave pattern using a ripple tank and a stroboscope

DESCRIBING WAVES

Reflection

Figure 8 shows some plane waves approaching a straight metal barrier. The barrier is big enough to prevent waves going 'over the top'. The incident waves are reflected from the barrier.

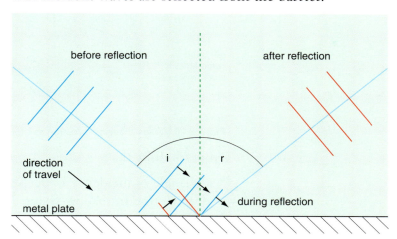

Figure 8 The reflection of waves off a plane surface – the angle of incidence = i, the angle of reflection = r

Note carefully that:

* the **angle of incidence always equals the angle of reflection**
* the wavelengths of incident and reflected waves are equal
* the frequency of the incident waves is the same as that of the reflected waves
* there is continuity of incident waves and reflected waves at the barrier.

The behaviour of water waves at a boundary is very similar to that of light at a mirror. However, water waves can be observed easily because they have a wavelength of many centimetres. Light waves have a wavelength typically around half a millionth of a metre, so their wave behaviour is a little more difficult to demonstrate.

Refraction

In Figure 9, water waves are travelling from deep water to shallow water. A region of shallow water in a ripple tank can be made by immersing a rectangular glass block. The block displaces the water so that the water directly above it is shallow while the surrounding water is deeper.

Waves travel more slowly in shallow water than they do in deep water. Since the same number of waves leave the deep water as enter the shallow water every second, the frequencies in the deep and shallow regions must be the same. This in turn means that the waves in shallow water must have a shorter wavelength than those in deep water.

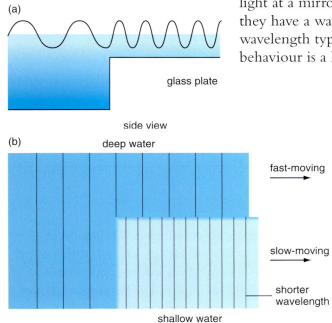

Figure 9 a Side view and **b** aerial view of waves going from a deep water area to a shallow water area

When water waves enter the shallow region obliquely (at an angle), they not only slow down, but also change direction as shown in Figure 10.

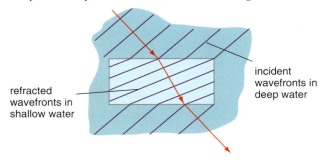

Figure 10 Waves changing direction as they pass from deep to shallow water

Note carefully that:

* the angle of incidence in deep water is always bigger than the angle of refraction in shallow water
* the wavelength and speed of waves in deep water are greater than that in shallow water
* the frequencies of waves in both deep and shallow water are the same
* there is continuity of incident and refracted waves at the boundary.

Example
A deep-water wave of wavelength 12 cm and speed 36 cm/s enters a shallow region where the wavelength is 8 cm. Find the wave speed in shallow water.

Answer

$$\text{frequency in deep water} = \frac{v}{\lambda}$$
$$= \frac{36}{12}$$
$$= 3\,\text{Hz}$$
$$\text{frequency in shallow water} = \text{frequency in deep water}$$
$$= 3\,\text{Hz}$$
$$\text{speed in shallow water} = f \times \lambda$$
$$= 3 \times 8$$
$$= \mathbf{24\,cm/s}$$

▶ Sound

Sound waves are produced when an object vibrates. The range of human hearing is around 20 Hz to 20 000 Hz (20 kHz), but this upper limit decreases with age. It is not unusual for middle-aged people to have an upper limit of around 15 000 Hz. Sound at frequencies above 20 kHz cannot be heard by humans and is called **ultrasound**.

The vibrating object causes small changes in air pressure that are passed from molecule to molecule as a longitudinal wave. In this way, energy passes from particle to particle by collisions, which explains why sound cannot travel through a vacuum, where there are no particles. Figure 11 shows an important experiment to demonstrate that sound needs a medium (material) to pass through.

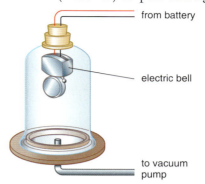

Figure 11 This experiment shows that sound cannot travel through a vacuum

The ringing electric bell is seen and heard from inside the bell jar. The pump is switched on and slowly the air is pumped out of the jar. As the air is removed, the sound becomes fainter and fainter until all the air has been removed, when it can scarcely be heard at all. Some sound will always be heard but this is the sound that travels through the supporting wires and outwards through the glass jar.

Table 2 gives some examples of what is vibrating when certain sounds are made. In every case the vibrating object causes the surrounding air to vibrate. This in turn causes sound to pass through the air to your ear. But without some medium such as the air, sound cannot reach your ear.

> **DID YOU KNOW?**
>
> Although the normal outdoor range of the human voice is 200 metres, the whistled language of the Spanish-speaking Canary Islanders of La Gomera can be heard more than 3 kilometres away.

Sound coming from …	What is vibrating?
Drum	Drum skin
Loudspeaker	Cone of the speaker
Human voice	Vocal cords in the larynx
Guitar	Strings
Clarinet	Reed
Bell	Gong

Table 2

Pitch, loudness and waveform

The easiest way to display the waveform of a sound is to use a microphone with a **cathode ray oscilloscope** (CRO). The microphone converts the sound into electrical energy, while the CRO gives a visual representation of the sound. Figure 12 shows how sound waves can be displayed on a CRO screen.

Figure 12 Displaying sound waves on a CRO screen

An oscilloscope allows us to see a 'picture' of a sound wave. If we look at the oscilloscope pattern for **a simple sound**, it will look like the screen in Figure 12.

The wave patterns in Figure 13 have the same amplitude of 2 units, so they have the same loudness. However, the wave patterns have different frequencies. Musicians use the word **pitch** to describe the frequency of a sound or musical note. Bass notes are low pitch, treble notes are high pitch. The pitch of a note is directly related to its frequency. The higher-pitched notes are those with higher frequencies.

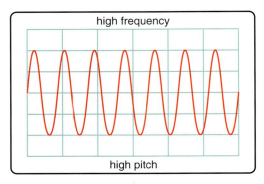
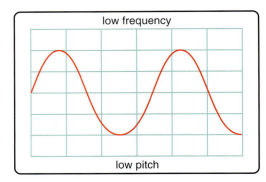

Figure 13 Increasing the frequency makes the peaks closer together – pitch increased

Loudness is linked to the energy of the sound wave reaching your ears. The louder the sound, the greater is its energy. We can relate the loudness of a sound wave to its amplitude.

The wave patterns shown in Figure 14 have the same pitch, but different loudness – the red wave has a bigger amplitude (3 units) than the blue wave (0.5 units), so the sound it represents is louder.

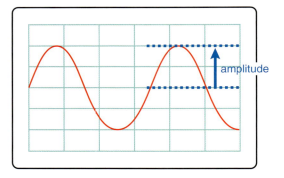
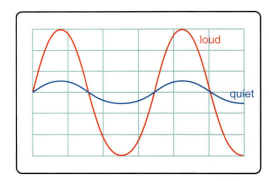

Figure 14 The effects of changing the loudness of a sound wave

Sound reflection

Like all waves, sound and ultrasound can be made to reflect. Reflected sound is called an **echo**.

This happens in a way that is similar to the reflection of water waves discussed earlier. It is important to remember that whenever waves reflect, the angle of incidence is *always* equal to the angle of reflection.

Figure 15 The reflection of sound waves from a surface

Ultrasound

Everybody knows that dogs can hear sounds from dog whistles that humans cannot detect. Bats too have the ability to hear very high-pitched sounds. This type of sound is called **ultrasound** because it is above the upper limit of human hearing – that means it is above 20 kHz.

Interestingly whales, dolphins, sharks and many other creatures that live in the sea are well-adapted to hearing both sound and ultrasound. The audible clicks that whales produce pass through the water easily from animal to animal. But many sea creatures can also produce and hear ultrasound, and use it for locating their prey.

In the past few years, biologists have discovered that elephants emit sounds that can travel incredible distances, especially at night. It is believed the elephants use this sound to communicate with each other, over distances of many kilometres. This sound has a frequency *below* that of human hearing and is called **infrasound**.

Man has found many applications for ultrasound:

* scanning metal castings for faults or cracks (e.g. in rail tracks)
* scanning a woman's womb to check on the development of a foetus
* scanning soft tissues to diagnose cancers
* fish location by seagoing trawlers
* mapping the surface of the ocean floor in oceanography
* cleaning sensitive electronic equipment
* removing harmful tartar from teeth.

> **DID YOU KNOW?**
>
> Whales are not only the largest mammals in the oceans – they are also the noisiest. They give out low-frequency sounds that can be detected by other whales thousands of kilometres away.

An application of ultrasound in medicine

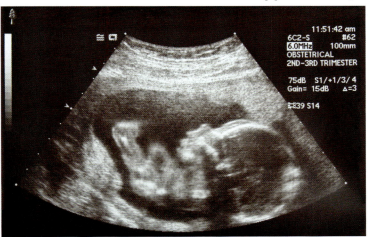

Figure 16 This ultrasound scan shows an unborn baby in its mother's womb

In an ultrasound scan of an unborn baby, a probe is moved across the mother's abdomen. The probe sends out ultrasound waves and also detects the reflections. The low wavelength of the ultrasound waves means that, unlike audible sound waves, ultrasound can be sent out in a very narrow beam and can easily be focused on the unborn baby. The other end of the probe is connected to a computer.

By examining the reflected waves from the womb, the computer builds up a picture of the foetus like that in Figure 16. Unlike X-rays, ultrasound is now known to be quite safe for this purpose.

An application of ultrasound in industry

People who study the structure of the Earth are called geologists. People who study physics are called physicists. Geophysicists are scientists with a training in both *geology* and *physics*. They travel all over the world to help search for vital materials like oil and minerals.

WAVES, SOUND AND LIGHT

Geophysicists can tell the structure of rocks by setting off explosions and listening to the echoes with a network of microphones. The sound waves both reflect and refract (bend) as they pass through different rock types. The idea is shown in Figure 17 – at the boundary between rocks A and B, refraction and reflection both take place.

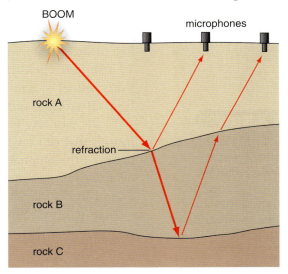

Figure 17 Investigating Earth's structure

From the way in which the sound refracts and reflects, geophysicists can tell if there is oil, gas, coal or other minerals deep underground. Only then is a decision made to drill a well or carry out mining.

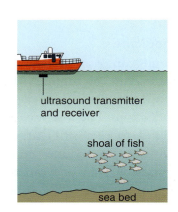

Examples

1 A fishing boat sends out an ultrasound pulse which travels in water at a speed of 1500 m/s to the shoal of fish. The time between the transmitted pulse and the received pulse is 0.2 seconds.

a) Calculate the total distance travelled by the ultrasound pulse.

b) Calculate the distance from the boat to the shoal of fish.

c) Shortly after the first ultrasound pulse is received, another echo is received at the boat. Explain.

Answer

a) Total distance travelled by pulse = speed × total time
$$= 1500 \times 0.2$$
$$= \mathbf{300\,m}$$

b) Distance from the boat to the shoal of fish = $\frac{1}{2}$ × total distance
$$= \frac{1}{2} \times 300$$
$$= \mathbf{150\,m}$$

c) The first ultrasound pulse received at the boat is the echo from the fish. The second ultrasound pulse received at the boat is the echo from the more distant sea bed.

2 Dolphins use sound underwater both to communicate and to locate.

Dolphin A sends out a pulse of sound to communicate with dolphin B. The sound takes 0.2 s to travel 300 m from dolphin A to dolphin B. Calculate the speed of sound in water.

Answer
$$\text{speed} = \frac{\text{total distance}}{\text{total time taken}}$$
$$= \frac{300}{0.2}$$
$$= 1500 \text{ m/s}$$

3 A golfer uses an ultrasonic device to measure the distance to the flag. The device shows that the distance is 82.5 m. If the speed of sound in air is 330 m/s, how long does it take for the sound to travel to the flag and back again?

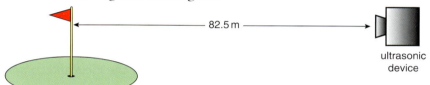

Answer
$$\text{time} = \frac{\text{total distance}}{\text{speed}}$$
$$= \frac{82.5 \times 2}{330}$$
$$= 0.5 \text{ s}$$

4 When John bangs two blocks of wood together, he hears an echo from a distant wall.

He bangs the blocks of wood together to make a clapping sound. After some practice, he is able to bang the blocks together at exactly the same time the echo reaches him.

John's assistant measures the time it takes John to complete 51 claps (50 time intervals). She measures this as 30 seconds. The distance from John to the wall is measured as 90 m.

Calculate the speed of sound from these measurements.

Answer
$$\text{time interval between claps} = \frac{30 \text{ seconds}}{50 \text{ claps}}$$
$$= 0.6 \text{ seconds}$$
$$\text{speed of sound} = \frac{\text{distance to wall and back}}{\text{time taken}}$$
$$= \frac{90 \times 2}{0.6}$$
$$= 300 \text{ m/s}$$

Questions

3 a) Why is a lightning flash generally seen before thunder is heard?
  b) If 4 seconds elapse between a lightning flash and the sound of thunder, approximately how far away is the storm? Take the speed of sound to be 330 m/s.

4 On a stormy night a fishing trawler sounds its foghorn and 6 seconds later the echo from a dangerous cliff is heard on board the ship. If the speed of sound is 330 m/s, how far is the cliff from the trawler?

5 The table below shows the results of an experiment to investigate how the wavelengths of sound change with different frequencies.

Frequency (Hz)	680	440	170	136	85	68
Wavelength (m)	0.5	1.0	2.0	2.5	4.0	5.0
1/Wavelength (m^{-1})			0.50		0.25	

  a) Copy the table and complete the last row.
  b) Plot the graph of frequency (y-axis) against 1/wavelength and draw the straight line of best fit.
  c) Circle on the graph the result that is probably incorrect.
  d) Use the graph to complete the following:
  The frequency of a sound is _____ to its 1/wavelength.
  e) Use the table or the graph to find the speed of sound.

6 The lines in the diagram opposite are the crests of straight water ripples moving to the right.
  a) Calculate the wavelength of the ripples.
  It takes 10 seconds for ripple A to move to the position now occupied by ripple F.

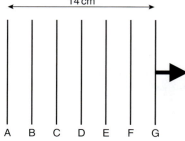

  b) Calculate the frequency of the ripples and their speed.

7 a) Copy and complete the table below to show what happens when water waves refract as they pass from deep water into shallow water. In the empty spaces write 'increases' or 'decreases' or 'does not change' as appropriate.

Property	Increases/Decreases/Does not change
Wavelength	
Frequency	
Speed	

  b) Add another column to your table and fill it in to show how the wavelength, frequency and speed of water waves change, if at all, when they reflect from a barrier.

Light

Reflection of light

All of us are familiar with the way light reflects from a straight (plane) mirror. The essential ideas are shown in Figure 18.

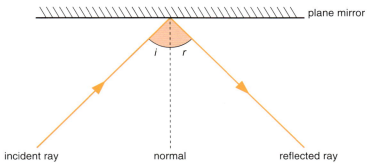

Figure 18 Reflection by a plane mirror

* The ray of light travelling towards the mirror is called the **incident ray**.
* The perpendicular to the mirror where the incident ray strikes it is called the **normal**.
* The ray that travels away from the mirror is called the **reflected ray**.
* The angle between the incident ray and the normal is called the **angle of incidence**, i.
* The angle between the reflected ray and the normal is called the **angle of reflection**, r.

Experiments show that the angle of incidence is always equal to the angle of reflection. This is known as the **law of reflection**. You should be able to describe an experiment to demonstrate this law.

Proving the law of reflection

1. With a sharp pencil and a ruler, draw a straight line AOB on a sheet of white paper using a ruler.
2. Use a protractor to draw a normal, N, at point O.
3. With the protractor, draw straight lines at various angles to the normal ranging from 15° to 75°.
4. Place a plane mirror on the paper so that its back rests on the line AOB.
5. Using a ray box, shine a ray of light along the line marked 15°.
6. Mark two crosses on the reflected ray on the paper.
7. Remove the mirror, and using a ruler join the crosses on the paper with a pencil and extend the line backwards to point O – this line shows the reflected ray.
8. Measure the angle of reflection with a protractor.
9. Record in a table the angles of incidence and reflection.
10. Repeat the experiment for different angles of incidence up to 75°.

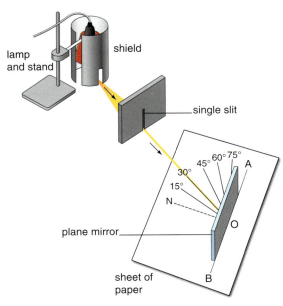

Figure 19 Experiment to demonstrate the law of reflection

Note that when light is reflected from a rough surface, such as paper, the law of reflection still applies. But the paper surface is rough (Figure 21) and the light is reflected in many different directions and cannot produce a clear image. This is called **diffuse reflection**.

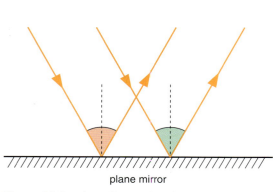

Figure 20 Regular reflection by a flat surface, such as a plane mirror

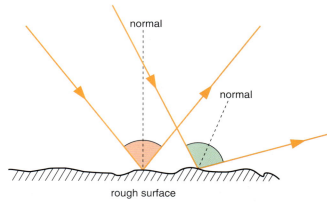

Figure 21 Diffuse reflection by a rough surface, such as a piece of paper

Where is the image we see in a plane mirror? We know it is behind the mirror, but how far behind? To answer that question we need to do another experiment.

Where is the image?

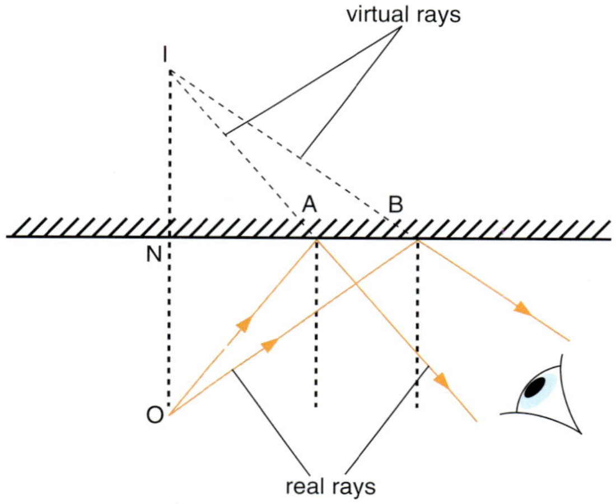

1. Support a plane mirror vertically on a sheet of white paper, and with a pencil draw a straight line at the back to mark the position of the reflecting surface.
2. Use a ray box to direct two rays of light from point O towards points A and B on the mirror.
3. Mark the position of point O with a cross using a pencil.
4. Mark two crosses on each of the real reflected rays.
5. Remove both the ray box and the mirror.
6. Using a ruler, join the crosses with a pencil line so as to obtain the paths of the real rays from A and B.
7. Extend these lines behind the mirror (these are called virtual rays) – they meet at I, the point where the image was formed.
8. Measure the distance from the image I to the mirror line (IN) and the distance from the object O to the mirror line (ON) – they should be the same.
9. Repeat the experiment for different positions of the object O.
10. In each case, the object O and its image I should be the same perpendicular distance from the mirror.

Figure 22 The image in a plane mirror is the same distance behind as the object is in front

> **DID YOU KNOW?**
>
> The human eye can detect light passing through a hole only three thousandths of a millimetre in diameter. But, that is nothing compared with some of the most powerful telescopes. They can detect the light from a candle at a distance of over 100 000 km!

LIGHT

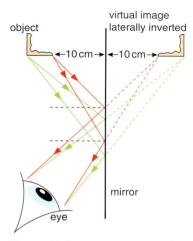

Figure 23 Seeing an image in a plane mirror

The image in a plane mirror

Figure 23 shows what happens when light from a point object strikes a mirror. The reflected rays get further apart (diverge) and enter the eye. But the eye follows the rays back in a straight line. The rays entering the eye appear to come from a point behind the mirror. This point is the **image**.

Note that the image in a plane mirror is not caused by *real* rays of light coming to a focus, as happens on a cinema screen. A mirror image is therefore called a **virtual** image.

A mirror image is also 'back-to-front'. If we hold a left-handed glove in front of a mirror, its image looks like a right-handed glove and vice versa. The image is said to be **laterally inverted**.

The image in a plane mirror is:

* virtual
* the same size as the object
* laterally inverted
* the same distance behind the mirror as the object is in front of the mirror.

Applications of plane mirrors

Plane mirrors are used:

* in looking glasses to see an image of ourselves

Figure 24 Using a plane mirror to obtain an image of oneself

* in simple periscopes to see over an obstacle – like seeing over the heads of other spectators at football matches
* in instruments where a pointer moves over a scale – for accurate readings the image of the pointer must be under the pointer itself.

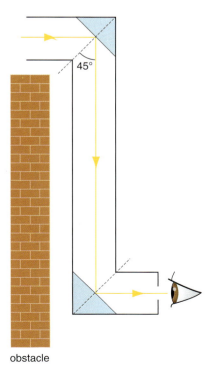

Figure 25 Using two plane mirrors in a periscope

Figure 26 The image of the pointer must be under the pointer itself

Questions

8. What size is the angle of incidence when the incident ray strikes a plane mirror at 90°?
9. The angle between a plane mirror and the incident ray is 40°. What size is the angle of reflection?
10. The angle between the incident ray and the reflected ray is 130°. What size is the angle of incidence?
11. Write the word 'AMBULANCE' in its laterally inverted form. Why is this laterally inverted form sometimes seen painted on real ambulances?
12. Two plane mirrors are inclined at right angles to each other. A ray of light strikes one mirror, M_1, at an angle of incidence of 30° and the reflected ray from M_1 falls incident on M_2. Find the angle of reflection at M_2. Comment on the direction of the ray incident on M_1 and the reflected ray from M_2.
13. A ray of light strikes a plane mirror so that the angle between the mirror and the ray is 90°. What size is the angle of incidence? In what direction is this ray reflected?

▶ Refraction of light

Material	Speed of light in m/s
Air (or vacuum)	300 000 000
Water	225 000 000
Glass	200 000 000

Table 3

Refraction is the change in direction of a beam of light as it travels from one material to another due to a change in speed in the different materials. Table 3 shows the speed of light in various media. It is not necessary to remember the numbers in this table, but you must know that light travels faster in air than in water, and faster in water than in glass.

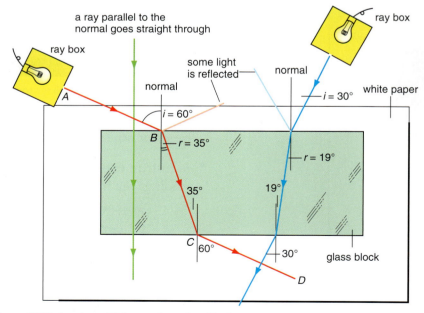

Figure 27 Refraction of light rays by a glass block

* The angle between the normal and the incident ray is called the **angle of incidence**.

* The angle between the normal and the refracted ray is called the **angle of refraction**.
* The angle between the normal and the emergent ray is called the **angle of emergence**.

Note:
* if the block has parallel sides, the angle of incidence is equal to the angle of emergence
* a ray parallel to the normal does not bend as it enters the block.

Experiments show that:
* when light speeds up, it bends away from the normal
* when light slows down, it bends towards the normal.

Remember that this is also what happens to waves travelling from deep water into shallow water.

Figure 28 shows what happens when light travels from air through glass, then through water, and finally back into the air. Note the changes of direction in each case.

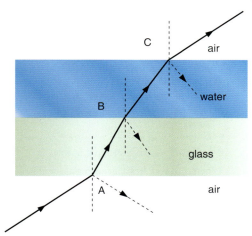

Figure 28 Refraction

As the light:

* enters the glass from the air at point A it slows down, so it bends *towards* the normal
* passes from glass into water at point B it speeds up a little, so it bends *away* from the normal
* passes from water into air at point C it speeds up even more, so it bends still more away from the normal.

Analogy between the behaviour of water waves and the behaviour of light

There are many similarities between the behaviour of water waves in a ripple tank and the behaviour of light. Both show reflection, in which the angle of incidence is equal to the angle of reflection. When water waves travel from deep water into shallow water they refract in exactly the same way as when light travels from air into glass. These similarities mean that we can say there is an *analogy* between light waves and water waves.

However, we can see much more happening when we look at the reflection and refraction of water waves than we can with light. For one thing, we can see that the wavelengths, frequencies and speed of the incident water waves are equal to the wavelengths, frequencies and speed of the reflected water waves. This led physicists to suspect that the wavelength, frequency and speed of light waves do not change when they reflect – and in fact this turns out to be the case.

By looking at the movement of floating chalk dust on the surface of water we can say with confidence that water waves are transverse. This leads us to think that light waves are transverse too – and, as we know, this is the case.

WAVES, SOUND AND LIGHT

But what does refraction tell us? When water waves refract as they pass from deep water to shallow water they bend towards the normal. This is exactly what happens when light passes from air into glass. When we measure the speed of water waves we find that deep water waves move faster than shallow water waves. If we apply the analogy again, then we would suspect that light travelling in air is moving faster than light travelling in glass. Once again, this turns out to be the case. The analogy is summarised in Table 4.

Water waves	Light
When they reflect: * angle of incidence = angle of reflection * reflected wavelength = incident wavelength * reflected frequency = incident frequency * reflected speed = incident speed	When it reflects: * angle of incidence = angle of reflection * reflected wavelength = incident wavelength * reflected frequency = incident frequency * reflected speed = incident speed
When they pass from deep into shallow water: * they bend towards the normal * refracted wavelength is less than incident wavelength * refracted frequency = incident frequency * refracted speed is less than incident speed	When it passes from air into glass and it refracts: * it bends towards the normal * refracted wavelength is less than incident wavelength * refracted frequency = incident frequency * refracted speed is less than incident speed

Table 4 Analogy between water waves and light

Sound refracts when it passes from water into the air as shown in Figure 29.

* What does this tell us about the speed of sound in water compared with its speed in air?
* What does this suggest about the molecules in water and the molecules in air?

Figure 29

Dispersion

All colours (frequencies) of light travel at the same speed in air. But different colours of light travel at different speeds in glass. This means that different colours bend by different amounts when they pass from air into glass. When light is passed through a triangular glass block, a **prism**, the effect is called **dispersion** and it results in a **spectrum** showing all the colours of the rainbow. Red light is bent (refracted) the least because it travels fastest in glass. Violet light bends the most because it is slowest in glass.

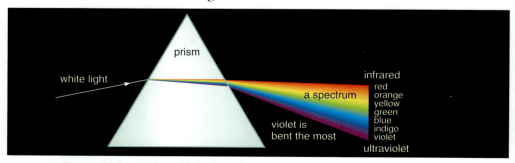

Figure 30 Dispersion of light through a prism

REFRACTION OF LIGHT

Total internal reflection

Figure 31 shows what happens when light travels through glass and emerges into the air. When the angle of incidence in glass is small enough, most of the light refracts into the air, but a little light is **internally** reflected.

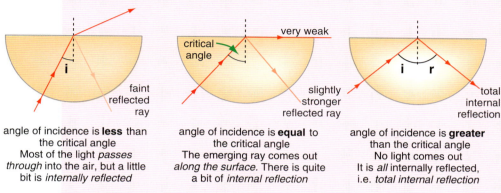

angle of incidence is **less** than the critical angle
Most of the light *passes through* into the air, but a little bit is *internally reflected*

angle of incidence is **equal** to the critical angle
The emerging ray comes out *along the surface*. There is quite a bit of *internal reflection*

angle of incidence is **greater** than the critical angle
No light comes out
It is *all* internally reflected, i.e. *total internal reflection*

Figure 31 Total internal reflection of light

As the angle of incidence increases, the refracted ray bends closer and closer to the glass and becomes weaker and weaker. At the same time, the light being internally reflected into the glass becomes stronger. Eventually, at a certain angle of incidence called the **critical angle**, the light is refracted at an angle of refraction of 90°. At this point the refracted ray is very weak and the internally reflected ray is quite strong.

The critical angle for glass is about 42°. At angles above the critical angle, there is no refraction at all. *All* the light is reflected back into the glass – this is called **total internal reflection**.

You should remember that:

* the critical angle is the angle of incidence in a material for which the angle of refraction in air is 90°

* at angles of incidence less than the critical angle, both reflection and refraction occur

* at angles of incidence greater than the critical angle, no refraction occurs and the light is totally internally reflected.

You are required to investigate experimentally the conditions under which total internal reflection occurs within parallel-sided glass blocks and triangular prisms.

The first condition is that the light must be travelling from glass (or Perspex) towards the air; the second is that the angle of incidence in the glass (or Perspex) must be greater than the critical angle.

Uses of total internal reflection

Total internal reflection is used in optical fibres for communications and keyhole surgery.

Optical fibres are lengths of solid glass core with an outer plastic sheath. Provided that the fibre is not bent too tightly, light will strike the core–cladding boundary at an angle greater than the critical angle and be totally internally reflected at the surface of the glass core. However, every optical fibre has some imperfections at its reflecting surface and this means that the signal must be boosted every kilometre or so in communications links. Optical fibres are used to transmit both telephone and video signals over long distances.

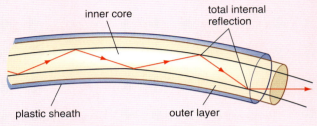

Figure 32 Passage of light through an optical fibre

The big advantage of optical fibres is that they can carry much, much more information than a copper cable of the same diameter. It has been estimated that the optical fibres in a sheath no thicker than a man's arm could carry all the telephone conversations taking place at any one time, all over the world.

What happens if the optical fibre is too tightly bent? If this happens, the angle of incidence at the core–cladding boundary may become less than the critical angle and light will be lost by refraction into the cladding.

Endoscopes are used by surgeons to look inside a patient's body without needing to cut a large hole. They consist of bundles of optical fibres that allow light to travel into the body and then allow image information to pass out of the body. The surgeon can therefore see on a monitor what is happening inside the body, as it happens. The endoscope kit also carries tools for cutting, snaring, water irrigation and retrieval of tissue. It is the use of optical fibres that makes keyhole surgery possible. Other examples of the use of total internal reflection include prism binoculars and the prism periscope.

Lenses

Lenses are specially shaped pieces of glass or plastic. There are two main types of lens:

* **converging** (or **convex**)
* **diverging** (or **concave**).

Figure 33 The shapes of a converging lens and a diverging lens

There are two features of a converging lens that need to be defined.

* Rays of light parallel to the principal axis of a **convex** (converging) lens all converge at the same point on the opposite side of the lens. This point lies on the principal axis and is called the **principal focus**.
* The distance between the principal focus and the optical centre of a lens is called the **focal length**.

Figure 34 shows how a convex lens refracts light. Note that light refracts at *each* surface as it enters and leaves the lens, first bending towards the normal and then away from the normal.

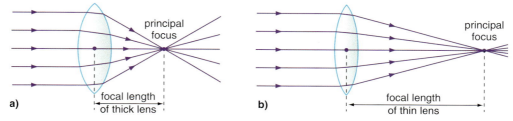

Figure 34 How light is refracted through a convex lens

There are two features of a diverging lens (Figure 35) that need to be defined.

* Rays of light parallel to the principal axis of a **concave** (diverging) lens all appear to diverge from the same point after refraction in the lens. This point lies on the principal axis and is called the **principal focus**.
* The distance between the principal focus and the optical centre of a lens is called the **focal length**.

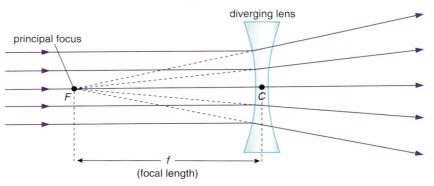

Figure 35 How light is refracted through a concave lens

Note that light passing through the optical centre of a convex or concave lens is not bent. It passes straight through without refraction. Of course, light can pass through a lens from left to right or from right to left, so every lens has two principal foci and two focal lengths. However, the only lenses you need to learn about at GCSE are equiconvex and equiconcave. This means that the principal foci on each side of the lens are the same distance from the optical centre. This becomes important when drawing ray diagrams to scale to find the position of an image.

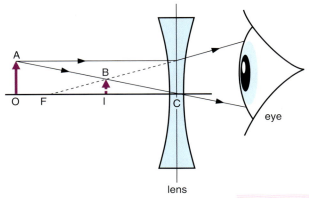

Note that regardless of the position of the object, the image in a concave (diverging) lens is *always*:

* erect
* virtual
* smaller than the object
* placed between the object and the lens.

This is shown in the ray diagram shown in Figure 36.

Figure 36 The image in a diverging lens

If you know the focal length of a lens and the position and height of an object, it is easy to draw a ray diagram to scale on graph paper to find the position and size of the image. To construct such a ray diagram you will need to draw at least two of the following rays:

* a ray parallel to the principal axis refracted through the principal focus
* a ray through the optical centre of the lens that does not change its direction
* a ray through the principal focus on one side of the lens, which emerges so that it is parallel to the principal axis on the other side of the lens.

How the image I is formed in a convex (converging) lens as the object O moves progressively away from the lens

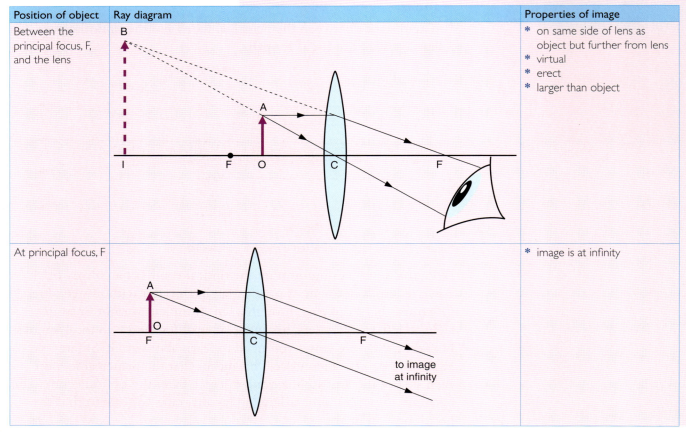

Position of object	Ray diagram	Properties of image
Between the principal focus, F, and the lens		* on same side of lens as object but further from lens * virtual * erect * larger than object
At principal focus, F		* image is at infinity

REFRACTION OF LIGHT

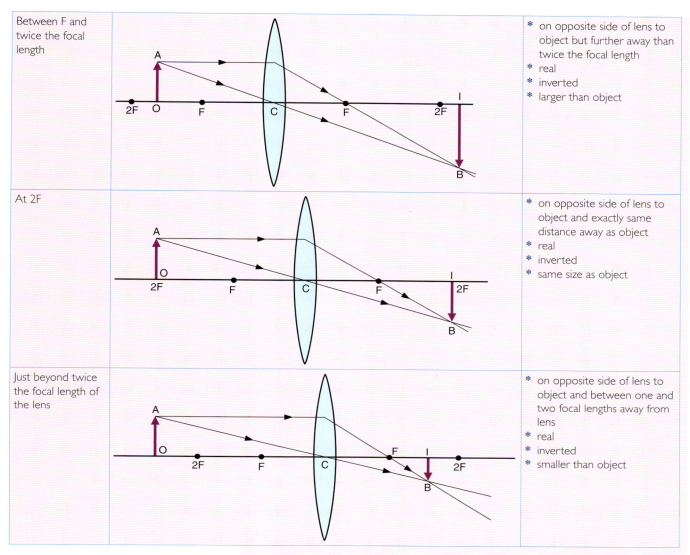

The results of these diagrams are summarised in Table 5.

Position of object	Location of image	Properties of image			Application
		Nature	Erect or inverted	Larger or smaller than object	
Between lens and F	On same side of lens as object, but further away from lens	Virtual	Erect	Larger	Magnifying glass
At F	At infinity	Real	Inverted	Larger	Searchlight
Between F and 2F	Beyond 2F	Real	Inverted	Larger	Cinema projector
At 2F	At 2F	Real	Inverted	Same size	Telescope – erecting lens
Just beyond 2F	Between F and 2F	Real	Inverted	Smaller	Camera
Very far away from lens	At F	Real	Inverted	Smaller	Camera

Table 5

> **DID YOU KNOW?**
>
> Probably the greatest scientist of the seventeenth century was Isaac Newton. But Newton was so frightened that his notes might fall into the hands of his rivals that he wrote them in code. Then, to make doubly sure, they were laterally inverted, as in a mirror.

When drawing ray diagrams, it is important to:

* draw a horizontal line to represent the principal axis and a vertical line for the lens
* mark the position of the principal focus with a letter F, the same distance from the optical centre on each side of the lens
* draw a vertical line touching the principal axis at the correct distance from the lens to represent the object
* draw at least two of the three construction rays, starting from the top of the object
* draw arrows on all rays to show the direction in which the light is travelling.

The point where the construction rays meet is at the top of the image. The bottom of the image lies vertically below on the principal axis.

To illustrate the process, consider the following example. An object 5 cm tall is placed 6 cm away from a converging lens of focal length 4 cm. Find the position and height of the image.

In the solution in Figure 37, circled numbers have been added to show the order in which the lines or rays have been drawn. These are drawn for illustration only and are normally omitted from such ray diagrams.

If the rays of light converge, the image is real and can be projected onto a screen.

In a converging lens it is useful to remember that:

* all real images are inverted – this means that if the object is drawn above the principal axis, the image will appear below the axis
* if the object is further away from the lens than the principal focus, the image will be real.

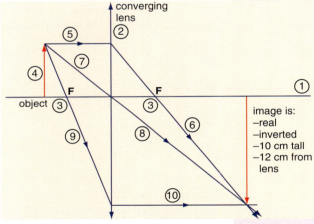

Figure 37 To work out the position and height of an image

But what happens if the rays that pass through the lens diverge? This happens when the object is placed closer to the lens than the principal focus. To locate the image, we trace the refracted rays backwards, in straight lines, to find the point where the refracted rays *appear* to come from. This point is the top of the image. It is conventional not to draw arrows on such construction lines because they are not rays at all, but simply lines drawn to locate the image. Such an image is virtual so it cannot appear on a screen. It is useful to remember that all virtual images formed by a converging lens are erect. This is the principle of the magnifying glass or simple microscope (Figure 38).

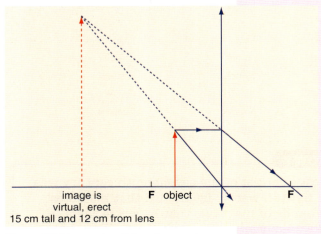

Figure 38 How a magnifying glass works

REFRACTION OF LIGHT

The camera

Figure 39 is a diagram of a simple camera being used to photograph a very distant object. Note that the light from such an object enters the camera lens as a parallel beam. The purpose of the lens is to project an image of a distant object onto a light-sensitive film.

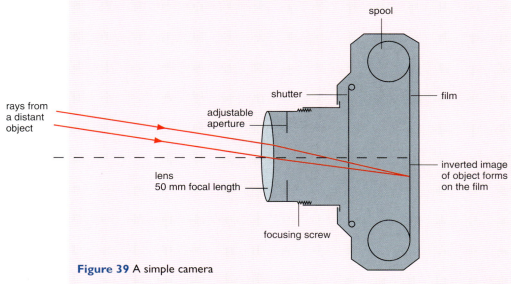

Figure 39 A simple camera

Focusing is achieved by changing the distance between the lens and the film. This is done by moving the lens backwards or forwards using the focusing screw.

Although film cameras are increasingly being replaced by digital cameras, the optical principles are very similar.

The projector

Because a projector has to produce an enlarged real image on a screen, the film or slide must be placed between one and two focal lengths away from the lens.

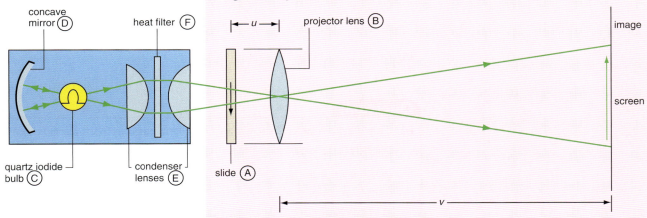

Figure 40 The principle of the slide projector

If the image on the screen is to be the right way up, the slide must be upside down when placed in front of the lens. Much of the design of a projector relates to the problem of getting rid of the heat coming from the projector's powerful lamp.

WAVES, SOUND AND LIGHT

Measuring the focal length of a convex lens experimentally

To carry out this experiment you need a metre ruler, a white screen and a convex lens in a suitable holder.

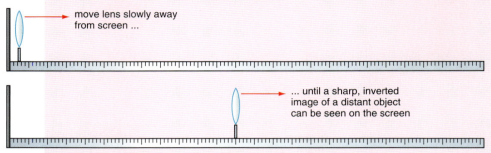

Figure 41 Measuring the focal length of a convex lens

* Tape the ruler to the bench and place the white screen at the zero mark.
* Place the lens in its holder as close as possible to the screen.
* Slowly move the lens away from the screen until the image of some distant object is as sharp as possible.
* Using the metre ruler, measure the distance from the centre of the lens to the screen – this distance is the focal length of the lens.

Rays of light from any point on a distant object arrive at the lens as a parallel beam. Such rays will be brought to a focus in the focal plane as shown in Figure 42. This is the plane at right angles to the principal axis and containing the principal focus.

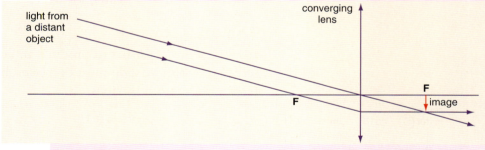

Figure 42

Questions

14 The diagram below shows a ray of light passing from air through two transparent media and back into air.

In which medium (air, A or B) is the light
i) fastest
ii) slowest?

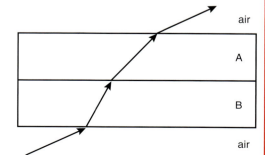

100

15 Sound is a wave that refracts as it passes from water into the air. The diagram shows an air–water boundary.

air
―――――――――――――
water

Sound is faster in water than it is in air. Copy the diagram and draw lines to show how a ray of sound refracts as it passes from water into the air.

16 A convex lens has a focal length of 6 cm. An object 4 cm tall is placed 3 cm from this lens.
   a) Draw to scale on graph paper an accurate ray diagram to show how the image is formed.
   b) How far is the image from the lens?
   c) Which three of the following words best describe the image?
      real, enlarged, erect, virtual, diminished, inverted

17 The convex lens in a camera is used to take a photograph of an object 36 cm away. The image is formed on a film 18 cm from the lens. By drawing on graph paper to a scale of 1:6, find the focal length of the lens.

▶ Electromagnetic waves

Electromagnetic waves are members of a family with common properties called the **electromagnetic spectrum**. They:

* can travel in a vacuum
* travel at exactly the same speed in a vacuum
* are transverse waves.

Electromagnetic waves also show properties common to *all* types of wave. They:

* carry energy
* can be reflected
* can be refracted.

There are seven members of the electromagnetic family. The properties of electromagnetic waves depend very much on their wavelength. In Table 6 they are arranged in order of increasing wavelength (or decreasing frequency).

Electromagnetic wave	Typical wavelength
Gamma (γ) rays	0.01 nm
X-rays	0.1 nm
Ultraviolet light	10 nm
Visible light	50 nm
Infrared light	0.01 mm
Microwaves or radar waves	3 cm
Radio waves	1000 m

1 nanometre (nm) = 1×10^{-9} m

Table 6 The electromagnetic spectrum

> **DID YOU KNOW?**
>
> The brightest known star is S-Doradus in the Magellan Clouds. It is thought to be about 50 times more massive than our Sun and about 1 million times brighter.

Uses and dangers of electromagnetic waves

Gamma (γ) rays, X-rays and ultraviolet light are known as **ionising radiations** because they convert atoms to charged ions as they pass through matter. This makes them much more dangerous than the others.

Gamma rays

Generally, waves with the shortest wavelengths (like γ waves) can destroy viruses and bacteria, disrupt the DNA in cells and cause cancers. These are also among the most penetrating radiations. They are therefore used in the treatment of tumours and in sterilising medical equipment such as plastic syringes and surgical dressings.

Gamma rays are also used in industry to detect leaks from underground pipes and to monitor the wear of machine parts like the piston rings in prototype car engines.

In the food industry, gamma rays are used to kill the surface fungi and bacteria that are present on fresh fruit and vegetables. This prolongs their shelf-life considerably and thus reduces costs and minimises waste.

X-rays

These too can cause cancers, so exposure to X-rays is always carefully controlled. They are widely used in medicine for diagnosis (finding out what is wrong) and for therapy (treatment). Although X-rays can pass through soft tissue like skin and muscle, most short wavelength X-rays are stopped by bone. This enables doctors to use them to take a photograph to check if a patient has a broken bone.

Slightly longer wavelength X-rays are used in body scanning. This enables the doctor to build up a picture of a section of the body (Figure 43).

Here the X-rays are not allowed to strike a photographic film. Instead they hit special sensors which pass their information to a computer so that the picture, or scan, is built up bit by bit. This type of scan is often used to investigate if a patient has cancer.

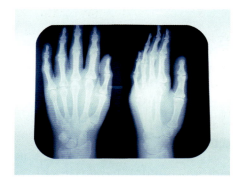

Figure 43 Longer wavelength X-rays are used to create an image of a complete scan through a person's body (1, 2 and 3 – heart, 4 – lungs, 5 – aorta, and 6 – spine).

Ultraviolet radiation

Objects that are extremely hot (above 4000°C) emit ultraviolet light. For people on Earth, the Sun is a major source of ultraviolet light. Prolonged exposure to ultraviolet radiation can cause skin cancer and damage to eyes. Sensible people always use a very high SPF (sun protection factor) cream when they are exposed to sunlight in the summer. Better still, they minimise exposure by spending more time in the shade.

Fortunately, much of the ultraviolet light from the Sun is absorbed by the **ozone layer** high above the Earth's surface. However, recent studies have shown that some pollutants are causing this layer to become very thin, particularly at high latitudes. Care will have to be taken if this effect is to be stopped and then reversed.

Ultraviolet light can be used to detect forgeries of banknotes. Special marks on banknotes are made with security ink and these only show up in ultraviolet light.

Water chillers also use an ultraviolet lamp to destroy the bacteria which might otherwise build up. Without this precaution, disease might spread in a contaminated water supply.

Visible light

Humans use visible light for vision and photography. However, probably the most important chemical reaction on Earth takes place as a result of the absorption of visible light – that reaction is **photosynthesis**. Photosynthesis is the process that happens in the leaves of green plants and causes the light energy to be converted into chemical energy in the form of starches and sugars.

Infrared radiation

All hot objects give out infrared radiation. Skin feels it as radiant heat. Infrared radiation is readily absorbed by objects, causing their temperature to rise. This makes it useful for toasters, grills, ovens and stoves.

Over-exposure to infrared radiation causes damage to cells. Infrared radiation causes burning of the skin (such as sunburn) but ultraviolet light causes skin cancer.

Infrared is used in night-vision equipment by detecting the radiation given off by living creatures or by engines. The hotter the object is, the brighter it appears in a night-vision scope. Night-vision scopes are mainly used by security forces and scientists interested in the behaviour of animals that are most active at night, such as badgers.

Infrared is also used for the remote controls of televisions, videos and car security systems. It is suitable for this purpose because it does not interfere with radio and television signals.

Figure 44 A night-vision scope detects infrared radiation given off by living creatures like these soldiers

Microwaves and radar waves

Microwaves and radar waves are essentially the same thing, but we give them different names to describe their use.

Microwaves of an appropriate wavelength are used for mobile phone and satellite transmissions because they readily pass through the Earth's atmosphere, including clouds. But the most common domestic use is the microwave oven. The microwaves pass easily into the food and are quickly absorbed by water molecules inside. Since our bodies contain a great deal of water, microwaves are a potential hazard. To minimise the risks, safety interlocks are fitted to the oven to prevent the production of microwaves when the door is open.

Air traffic controllers, pilots and the masters of large ships also use microwaves, as radar waves, for navigation. Increasingly too, motorists are making use of global positioning satellites (GPS) to find the best routes around and between large cities.

GPS are geosynchronous satellites that orbit the Earth at such a height and speed that they appear to be stationary to an observer on Earth. They are ideal to give the user a 'fix' concerning their position on the surface.

Microwaves are also used with optical fibres in intercontinental telecommunications and for cable TV.

Figure 45 Increasingly, people are using global positioning satellites to find their way around

WAVES, SOUND AND LIGHT

Radio waves

Radio waves are used extensively for communication. Television and FM radio use short wavelength radio signals, typically about 1 m long. This is why your television set can be tuned to receive some radio programmes. Radio communication is also important for pilots, seafarers, policemen and the military.

Health risks associated with mobile phones and communication masts

Mobile phones work by dividing a country into areas (called cells) each about 10–15 km wide. Each cell has its own microwave transmitter and receiver. When a call is made, rapid computer switching passes the call from one cell to another until it finally reaches the cell where the phone being called is to be found. The presence of so many microwave masts for mobile phones throughout the country has caused some people to link mobile phones with cancer. Others claim that because mobile phones use microwaves, holding the phone close to your ear can cause the brain to be damaged.

To investigate these claims, a committee, known as the Independent Expert Group on Mobile Phones, chaired by Sir William Stewart FRS, was asked by the British government to investigate and make recommendations. This high-powered group of experts reported that there is no proven case of damage being done to people either by communication masts or mobile phones. Nevertheless, they recommended that children under the age of nine should use mobile phones very sparingly, because their small body mass would make any possible harm to them more severe. The full report is available on the web at http://www.iegmp.org.uk/report/text.htm.

Search
- dispersion + light
- reflection
- electromagnetic + wave
- refraction
- light
- sound
- longitudinal
- transverse
- pitch + sound
- ultrasound
- rarefaction
- waves

Questions

18 Prolonged exposure to ultraviolet light can cause skin cancer.
   a) State two ways in which a person can reduce their risk of skin cancer due to ultraviolet light.
   b) State two uses for ultraviolet light, other than producing a sun-tan.
19 Infrared light is used in TV remote controls.
   a) State two other uses of infrared light in the home.
   b) In what way can infrared light cause harm?
20 State two properties that are unique to electromagnetic waves.
21 Which of the following types of electromagnetic radiation have:
   a) the longest wavelength
   b) the highest frequency?
      infrared, microwaves, radio waves, ultraviolet light, X-rays
22 The distance from a radio station to Belfast is 900 km. A radio signal of wavelength 1500 m and frequency 200 kHz is transmitted from the radio station. How long after transmission does it arrive in Belfast?

Exam questions

1 a) The diagram below shows two buoys, 60 m apart, floating on the sea.

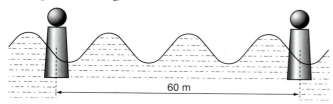

   i) Use the diagram to determine the wavelength of the sea waves. *(1 mark)*
   ii) Explain the meaning of the term 'frequency'. *(1 mark)*
   iii) Ten complete waves pass the buoy in 25 seconds. Calculate the frequency of the waves. *(1 mark)*
   iv) Calculate the speed of the waves across the sea. *(1 mark)*

b) Waves approaching a sea wall are shown below.

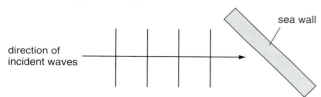

The arrow showing the direction of the incident waves is shown.
   i) Copy the diagram and draw another arrow showing the direction of the reflected waves. *(1 mark)*
   ii) On your diagram draw three waves that have been reflected from the sea wall. *(2 marks)*
   iii) Some distance from the sea wall, the waves come closer together. Explain. *(2 marks)*

2 a) The following objects are all producing sound.

   i) What are all of the objects doing to produce sound? *(1 mark)*
   ii) The drum is hit harder and this produces louder sound. What is happening to the drum skin to make the sound louder? *(1 mark)*
   iii) The loudspeaker is made to produce a higher-pitched sound. What is happening to the loudspeaker cone to make the pitch higher? *(1 mark)*

b) At an airport, the ground control officer wears ear protectors to protect his ears when he is near to the aircraft.
   i) What damage could be caused to his ears if he did not wear ear protectors? *(1 mark)*
   ii) Suggest one measure that could reduce the effects of noise pollution for people living in houses close to the airport. *(1 mark)*

c) Different waves form the electromagnetic spectrum.

radio waves   **visible light**
microwaves   **ultraviolet**   **infrared**
X-rays   **gamma waves**

Copy and complete the table by matching the statements to the correct waves above. *(3 marks)*

Statement	Waves
These waves can cause sunburn and skin cancer	
These waves can heat food	
These waves have the greatest wavelength	

3 a) The diagram shows a ray of white light incident on a glass prism. The prism breaks the white light up into a spectrum.

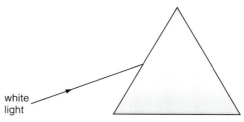

   i) What name is given to the breaking up of white light into different colours? *(1 mark)*
   ii) Copy and complete the ray diagram to show the paths taken by a ray of red light and a ray of violet light that result from the break-up of the white light as it enters the prism. *(2 marks)*
   iii) Explain what causes the glass prism to break white light up into its many colours. *(2 marks)*

b) In a camera, a lens is used to form an image of a film. The diagram below is full-scale and represents the lens of the camera and the film. The diagram shows an object in front of the camera lens. The lens is correctly adjusted so that a sharp image is formed on the film.

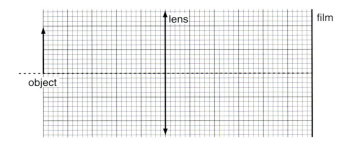

i) Copy the diagram onto graph paper and draw two rays of light from the top of the object to show how the image is formed on the film. *(2 marks)*

ii) Mark carefully and accurately the principal focus of this lens. *(1 mark)*

iii) Measure the focal length of the lens. *(1 mark)*

iv) Here is a list of properties of an image – **magnified, diminished, same size as object, same way up as object, upside down.** Which apply to the image formed on the film of this camera? *(3 marks)*

4 Tom and Sean are on a flat beach, some distance from a tall, vertical cliff as shown below.

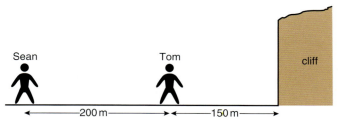

Sean was some distance from his friend Tom when he called out to him.
Tom heard his shout twice.

a) With the aid of the diagram above explain how this could have happened. *(2 marks)*

Tom is 150 m from the cliff and 200 m from Sean as shown in the diagram.
The speed of sound in air is 340 m/s.

b) Calculate the time interval between the two shouts heard by Tom. *(5 marks)*

5 Andrea uses a stretched slinky spring to demonstrate waves.

a) What types of wave are A and B in the diagram below? *(2 marks)*

b) What do both waves transfer as they move from left to right? *(1 mark)*

c) How does point X move as wave A passes along the slinky? *(2 marks)*

d) What is the amplitude of wave A in metres? *(1 mark)*

e) What is the wavelength of wave A? *(1 mark)*

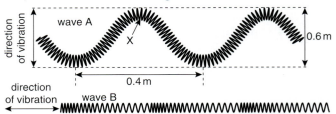

The end of wave A vibrates 30 times in 10 seconds.

f) What is the frequency of the wave? *(1 mark)*

g) Use your answers to parts **e)** and **f)** to calculate the speed of wave A in m/s. *(3 marks)*

6 a) All electromagnetic waves are transverse.
i) Explain what is meant by a 'transverse' wave. *(2 marks)*
ii) The table below gives the names of some electromagnetic waves.
Copy the table and draw arrows to match the wave with its use. One arrow has been drawn for you. *(5 marks)*

Electromagnetic wave	Use
X-rays	Kills cancer cells
Ultraviolet light	Detects banknote forgeries
Infrared light	Fast-food preparation
Gamma waves	Detects broken bones
Radio waves	Long distance communications
Microwaves	Night-time photography

7 Two mirrors, M_1 and M_2, are placed at right angles to one another. The diagram below shows a ray of light incident on mirror M_1 at an angle of 27° to its surface.

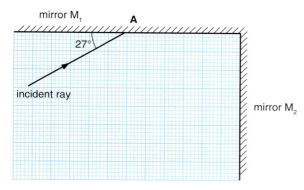

a) Copy the diagram onto graph paper and draw the normal to mirror M_1 at point A. *(1 mark)*

b) Calculate the angles of incidence and reflection at point A. *(2 marks)*

c) On your diagram draw, as accurately as you can, the reflected wave from A and from mirror M_2. *(2 marks)*

6 Electricity

Electricity is an extremely versatile and useful form of energy. Many of our everyday activities depend on the use of electricity. Living in society today would be unimaginable without it. Simple activities such as entertainment, communications, transport and industry would simply grind to a halt if electricity ceased to exist.

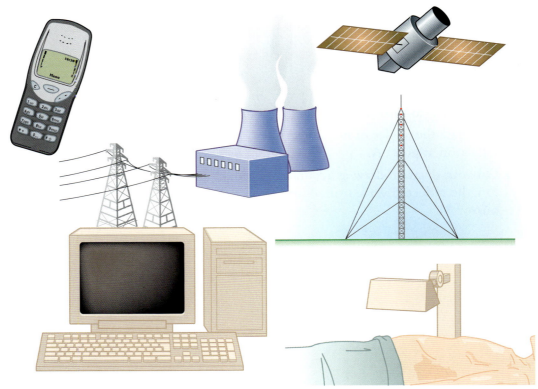

Figure 1 Without electricity life would be unimaginable

▶ Electrostatics

When a woollen jumper is taken off over a nylon shirt in the dark, you can hear crackles and see tiny blue electric sparks. The nylon shirt has become charged with **static electricity**.

Nature provides much more spectacular electrical discharges in the form of lightning.

There are two types of charge which can be demonstrated by the simple experiments shown in Figure 2.

When a polythene rod is rubbed with a cloth, electrons are taken off the cloth (which now has a shortage of electrons and is therefore positively charged) and transferred to the polythene rod (which now has a surplus of electrons and is therefore negatively charged).

In Figure 2a, the polythene rod has been rubbed with a cloth and suspended. When a second similarly charged polythene rod is brought up to the first one, the two rods repel each other.

ELECTROSTATICS

In Figure 2b, a rubbed cellulose acetate rod is brought close to the polythene rod. This time attraction occurs between the two rods.

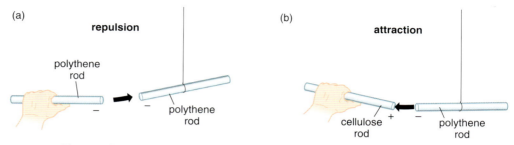

Figure 2 These two experiments demonstrate the existence of positive and negative charges

These simple experiments show that:

* there must be two types of charges – positive and negative – because there are two types of force
* bodies may be charged by friction.

The charge on cellulose acetate is taken as **positive** (+) and that on polythene is **negative** (−).

From the experiment, we can see that similar charges (i.e. + and +; or − and −) repel, while opposite charges (+ and −) attract. This can be summarised as:

> LIKE charges REPEL
> UNLIKE charges ATTRACT

So where do these charges come from, and why can the rods become oppositely charged? Scientists believe that atoms consist of a tiny positively charged nucleus surrounded by orbiting electrons, which are negatively charged.

When a cellulose acetate rod is rubbed with a cloth, electrons move from the cellulose acetate rod, leaving it positively charged, and the cloth gains electrons making it negatively charged.

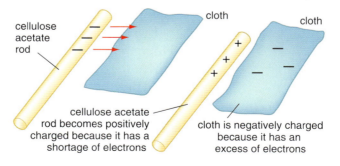

Figure 4 The rod has lost electrons and become positively charged – the cloth has gained the electrons and become negatively charged

It is important to remember that an object becomes negatively charged when it *gains* electrons and positively charged when it *loses* electrons.

> **DID YOU KNOW?**
> The static build-up in the home can lead to shocks of 50 000 V. However, very little harm is done because very few electrons flow.

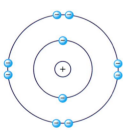

Figure 3 The 'satellite' model of an atom, with a central nucleus and orbiting electrons

ELECTRICITY

Charged objects can attract uncharged objects – for example, the charged screen of a television attracts dust. This effect may be explained by considering Figure 5 below.

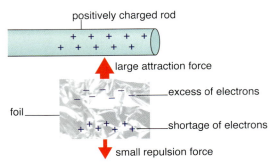

Figure 5 A charged object attracts an uncharged one

When a positively charged rod is brought near a tiny piece of aluminium foil, the free electrons in the foil are pulled towards the rod, creating a surplus of electrons at the top of the foil. The result is a deficiency of electrons at the bottom of the foil – i.e. a net positive charge is created at the bottom of the foil.

Consequently, the top of the foil is attracted to the rod, because unlike charges attract. But like charges repel, so the positive charges at the bottom of the foil are repelled. The attraction forces are stronger than the repulsion forces because the attracting charges are closer to the rod than the repelling charges. As a result there is a net upward attraction force between the rod and the foil.

Similarly, a charged polythene strip attracts an uncharged stream of water.

Useful applications of static electricity
Smoke precipitators in power stations

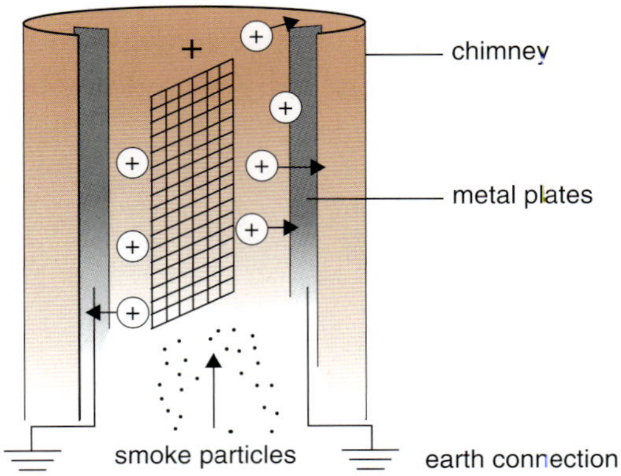

When fossil fuels are burned in power stations, vast quantities of smoke are emitted into the atmosphere along with the waste gases. Because the smoke consists of lots of tiny particles of solid matter, it can be removed from the chimneys before it passes out into the air using the principle of electrostatics.

In a device called a smoke precipitator, like that shown in Figure 6, the smoke particles pass up through the chimney, where they pass a negatively charged grid. As they pass the grid, they become negatively charged and so are repelled by it. The chimney is lined with large positively charged collecting plates which are connected to Earth. The negatively charged smoke particles are attracted to the oppositely charged plates, and as they touch them they lose their charge and fall to the bottom of the chimney, from where they can be collected.

Figure 6 A smoke precipitator in a fossil fuel power station

Photocopiers

Certain substances are electrical insulators in the dark, but become electrical conductors when exposed to light. These substances are called

photoconductors and include selenium, arsenic and tellurium. Use is made of photoconductors in photocopiers.

Paint spraying

In an electrostatic paint spray gun, like that shown in Figure 7, the droplets of paint become charged as they leave the gun. Because they are all given the same charge, they repel each other, forming a fine mist of paint. This results in an even coating on the object being painted. The process is made more efficient if the object is given an opposite charge to that of the paint droplets.

Figure 7 An electrostatic paint spray gun

Dangers of static electricity

Fuelling aircraft

When large petrol tankers are used to refuel aircraft, friction from the movement of the petrol through the pipe results in a charge on the pipe. If this charge were allowed to build up, it could be hazardous because of the flammable nature of the liquid. To prevent this, a wire connects the pipe nozzle to the ground, enabling the charges to leak away to Earth.

Figure 8 Refuelling an aircraft

Lightning

In a storm, if a cloud with a large charge comes close to a tall object on the ground – such as a building or a tree – the charge can run to Earth, resulting in a lightning strike. The air particles between the cloud and the tree become ionised. Some lose their electrons to become positive ions while others gain electrons to become negative ions. These ionised air particles allow the electrons to move quickly from the charged cloud to the tree during the discharge. The lightning flash is created when the air particles rejoin their missing charge.

Figure 9 Lightning between oppositely charged clouds

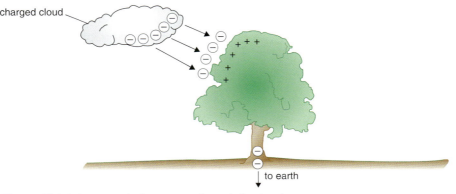

Figure 10 A lightning strike between a charged cloud and a tree

Overhead power cables

The overhead power cables that carry electricity around the country consist of insulated metal wires held high above the ground by insulated pylons. If a kite is flown too close to these uninsulated wires, an electric circuit would be completed, enabling the current to flow from the wires down to Earth through the person. The charge can be so large that it can easily kill the person holding the kite.

Figure 11 The insulated supports are clearly visible on these pylons

Static electricity as a nuisance

Static electricity can cause:

* clothes to stick together when removed from a tumble drier
* the moving black plastic handrails on an escalator to provide nasty 'shocks'
* 'shocks' from walking across a nylon carpet and then touching a door handle
* the need for the smart card in the satellite receiver to be 'discharged' occasionally due to the build-up of static charge
* TV screens and computer monitors to develop a build-up of static charge – they need to be cleaned frequently with antistatic cloths.

Questions

1. a) What is static electricity?
   b) Name the two types of charge.
   c) Write down the laws of forces between charged bodies.

2. a) Explain in terms of electron movement what happens when a polythene rod becomes negatively charged when rubbed with a cloth.
   b) What is the name of the process you have described in part a)?

3. A small positively charged polystyrene bead hangs on a nylon thread. Different rods are charged by friction and brought near the bead. The movement of the bead is recorded in a table. Copy the table and tick (✓) each charge present on the rod.

Material of rod	Bead movement	Charge on rod		
		Positive	Negative	Uncharged
Perspex	Repelled			
Cellulose acetate	Repelled			
Polythene	Attracted			
Steel	None			

4. Describe two examples where static electricity:
   a) is useful
   b) is a nuisance
   c) is dangerous.

Current electricity

An electric current is a flow of electric charge. When a Van der Graaf generator is connected to earth via a sensitive current meter, a current is detected by the meter.

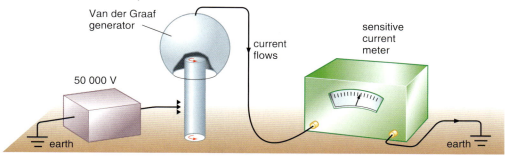

Figure 12

In metals the charge is carried by electrons. Most materials conduct electricity to a greater or lesser extent.

Very good conductors (plenty of free electrons)	Semi-conductors	Poor conductors (insulators) (very few free electrons)
Silver	Silicon	Plastic
Copper	Germanium	Wood
Steel		Rubber
Aluminium		Cork

Table 1 Classifying some common materials in terms of electrical conduction

Current in a simple circuit

An electric **cell** (commonly called a **battery**) can make electrons move – but only if there is a conductor connecting its two terminals making a complete circuit. Chemical reactions inside the cell push electrons from the negative (−) terminal round to the positive (+) terminal. Figure 13 shows how an electric current would flow in a wire connected across a cell.

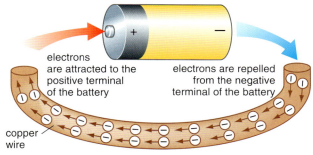

Figure 13 The flow of electrons in a simple cell

Electrons are repelled from the negative terminal of the cell, because like charges repel, and are attracted to the positive terminal, because unlike charges attract. The electrons therefore flow from the negative terminal to the positive terminal.

Scientists in the nineteenth century thought that an electric current consisted of a flow of positive charge from the positive terminal of the cell to the negative terminal. Unfortunately, although this idea is now known to be incorrect, this is still known as the direction of **conventional current**.

ELECTRICITY

Circuit diagrams and symbols

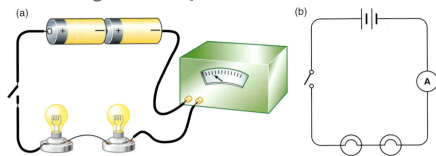

Figure 14 This circuit can be represented as a simple circuit diagram, using symbols for the different components

An electrical circuit may be represented by a **circuit diagram** with symbols for components. Circuit diagrams are easy to draw and are universally understood.

Component	Symbol	Component	Symbol
cell		ammeter	—(A)—
battery		voltmeter	—(V)—
wire	————	diode	
switch		variable resistor	
lamp		thermistor	
resistor		light dependent resistor (LDR)	
bell		buzzer	

Table 2 Components and their symbols

Measuring current

Ammeters, like those shown in Figure 15, are connected in circuits to measure current.

Figure 15b An analogue ammeter and a digital ammeter

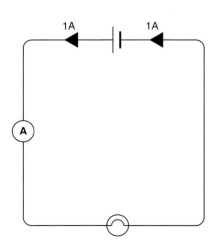

Figure 15a An ammeter connected in a simple circuit

An ammeter must be connected the correct way round. The red (+) terminal should be on the same side of the circuit as the positive (+) terminal of the battery. Putting an ammeter into a circuit has almost no effect on the current.

CURRENT ELECTRICITY

The relationship between charge and current

The unit of charge is the **coulomb** (C). If it were possible to see a coulomb of charge, it would look like a very large assembly of electrons – about six million million million of them.

The unit of current is the **ampere** (A). Currents of around 1 ampere upwards can be measured by connecting an ammeter in the circuit. For smaller currents, a **milliammeter** is used. The unit in this case is the milliampere (mA). (1000 mA = 1 A). An even smaller unit of current is the **microampere** (μA). (1 000 000 μA = 1 A)

The relationship between charge and current can be stated as follows:

> A current of 1 ampere is flowing when 1 coulomb of charge flows past a point in a circuit in 1 second. This is given by the formula:
>
> $$\text{charge} = \text{current} \times \text{time}$$
> $$\text{(C)} \qquad \text{(A)} \qquad \text{(s)}$$

For example, if a current of 5 A is flowing in a circuit, then 5 C of charge passes every point in 1 second.

In general, if a steady current I amperes flows for time t seconds, the charge Q coulombs passing any point is given by:

$Q = I \times t$

> **Example**
> A current of 150 mA flows around a circuit for 1 minute. How much electrical charge flows past a point in the circuit in this time?
>
> **Answer**
> $I = 150$ mA
> $\quad = 0.15$ A
> $t = 1$ minute
> $\quad = 60$ s
> $Q = I \times t$
> $\quad = 0.15 \times 60$
> $\quad = \mathbf{9\,C}$

There are two conditions which *must* be met before an electric current will flow:

* There must be a *complete circuit* – i.e. there must not be any gaps in the circuit.

* There must be a *source of energy* so that the charge may move – this source of energy may be a cell, a battery or the mains power supply.

ELECTRICITY

> **Questions**
> 5 Convert the following currents into milliamperes:
>   a) 3.0 A   b) 0.2 A
> 6 Convert the following currents into amperes:
>   a) 400 mA   b) 1500 mA
> 7 What charge is delivered if:
>   a) a current of 6 A flows for 10 seconds
>   b) a current of 300 mA flows for 1 minute?
> 8 Calculate the currents that flow when the following charges pass a point in the following times:
>   a) 100 C, time = 5 s   b) 500 mC, time = 50 s
>   c) 60 μC, time = 200 s.

▶ Potential difference, electromotive force and voltage

A battery, or cell, gives energy to the charge that passes through it. The ability of the cell or battery to do this is called the **potential difference** (PD) of the battery, usually called its **voltage**. The unit for PD and voltage is the **volt** (V).

A single AA cell has a PD of 1.5V. This means that each coulomb of charge that leaves the cell receives 1.5 joules of electrical energy. A PP3 battery with a PD of 9V will give 9 joules of energy to each coulomb of charge that leaves it. In other words, the bigger the PD of the cell, the more energy is given to each coulomb of charge.

What does the charge do with this energy?

Example 1 – the charge deposits this energy in the light bulb, which then converts the energy to light and heat.

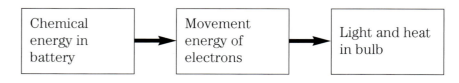

Figure 16

Example 2 – the charge deposits this energy in the motor, which then converts the energy to movement and heat.

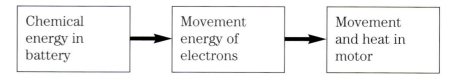

Figure 17

These two examples show that electric circuits behave like machines. They transfer electrical energy from one place to another or convert energy from one form to another.

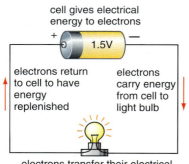

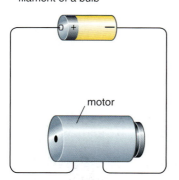

POTENTIAL DIFFERENCE, ELECTROMOTIVE FORCE AND VOLTAGE

A cell produces its highest PD when off-load – i.e. not supplying a current. This maximum PD is called the **electromotive force** (EMF) of the cell. However, when current is being supplied, the PD drops because of energy wastage inside the cell. For example, a car battery labelled '12 V' might only deliver 10 V when being used to turn a starter motor.

Cells in series

Portable stereo systems have a number of cells connected in series. The reason for this is that the system requires a large voltage to operate. Connecting cells in series to make a battery increases the voltage.

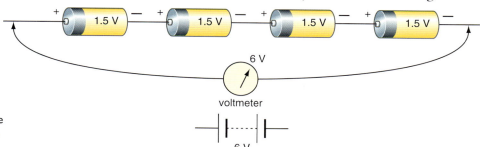

Figure 18 The voltage of a circuit can be increased by connecting cells in series to make a battery

You must be careful when connecting cells in series. If the polarity of one of the cells is reversed then the voltage is reduced, dramatically. The EMFs of two of the cells cancel each other out, leaving only one effective cell, as illustrated in Figure 19.

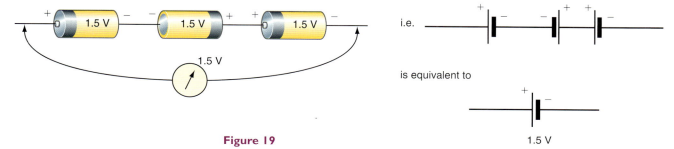

Figure 19

Potential differences around a circuit

In Figure 20, the electrons collect energy from the battery and deposit some of this energy in the light bulb and the rest of it in the electric motor. All the energy supplied by the battery is transformed in the bulb and motor. Almost none is spent in the connecting wires.

Like the battery, the bulb and motor each have a PD across them. A PD of 2V across the bulb means that each coulomb of charge that passes through the bulb deposits 2 joules of energy.

A PD of 4V across the motor means that each coulomb of charge that passes through the motor deposits 4 joules of energy.

The battery has a PD of 6V across it, because it supplies 6 joules of energy to each coulomb of charge that passes through it. Cells and batteries supply *energy* to the charge – they do not supply charge.

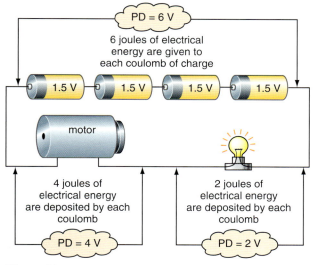

Figure 20

ELECTRICITY

Figure 21 shows the circuit diagram for the circuit in Figure 20. Note the voltage readings – they illustrate an important principle, which applies to any circuit:

> The sum of the PDs across the components is equal to the PD across the battery.

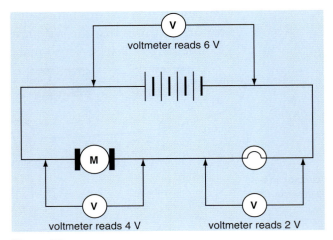

Figure 21

The relationship between charge, energy and voltage

There is a relationship between the voltage across a component and the charge flowing through it.

The voltage, measured in volts, is the ratio of the amount of energy, measured in joules, delivered by a cell or battery or deposited in a component per unit charge flowing through it.

$$\text{voltage} = \frac{\text{energy}}{\text{charge}}$$

In terms of units, this formula may be written as:

$$\text{volts} = \frac{\text{joules}}{\text{coulombs}}$$

When doing calculations, this triangle may be useful:

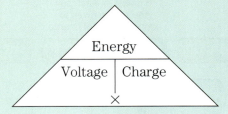

Questions

9 A cell is labelled '2V'. How many joules of energy are supplied to each coulomb of charge that the cell supplies?

10 A cell supplies 9 joules of energy to 6 coulombs of charge. What is the voltage of the cell?

11 How many joules of energy are deposited in a light bulb which has a PD of 18V across it when 3 coulombs of charge pass through it?

12 An electric motor consumes 150 joules of energy when 25 coulombs of charge pass through it. Find the PD across the motor.

13 The circuit below contains a 12V battery, a bulb and a motor.

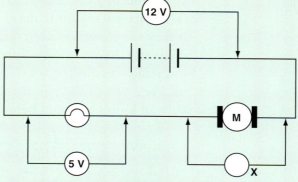

a) What type of meter is meter X?
b) What is the reading on meter X?
c) How many joules of electrical energy does each coulomb of charge possess as it leaves the battery?
d) How much electrical energy is deposited by each coulomb of charge as it passes through the motor?

▶ Series and parallel circuits

There are two types of electric circuits – **series circuits** and **parallel circuits**.

Series circuits

In a series circuit, the components are connected one after the other. There is only one path for the current to follow. If we measured the current at points 1, 2 and 3 in the circuit in Figure 22, it would have the same value. It is a common misconception to think that the current is used up. This cannot happen because electrons cannot disappear.

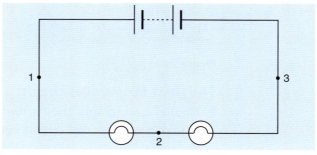

Figure 22 A series circuit

The bulbs share the PD from the battery. Because the PD is shared, the bulbs will not glow as brightly as they would if there were only one bulb in the circuit. The important thing to remember about series circuits is that if one bulb is removed, the other bulb(s) goes out because there is a break in the circuit – i.e. the circuit is no longer complete.

The rules for series circuits
* The current is the same everywhere in a series circuit.
* The components share the PD (voltage).

Parallel circuits

The lights in a house are usually connected in parallel. The reason for this is that each light requires the full mains voltage to work properly. If they were connected in series, the PD would be shared between them and they would be dimmer.

Parallel circuits (Figure 23) have junctions where the current splits up. Each part of the current then proceeds through the corresponding bulb and joins up again before going back to the battery.

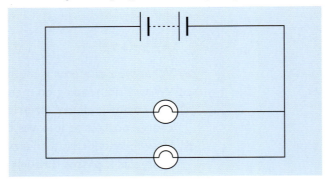

Figure 23 A parallel circuit

Because each bulb is connected directly to the battery, it receives the same PD – the bulbs therefore glow brightly. One major advantage of parallel circuits is that if one bulb is disconnected, the other bulbs in the circuit are unaffected. A second advantage of connecting bulbs in parallel is that the bulbs may be switched on and off independently (Figure 24).

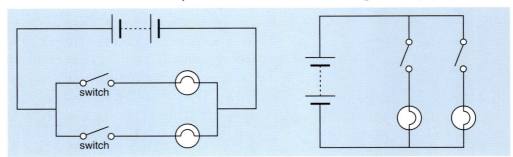

Figure 24

The rules for parallel circuits
* Parallel circuits split the current – the sum of the currents in the branches of a parallel circuit equals the current entering or leaving the junctions.
* The PD (voltage) across each component is the same.

▶ Resistance

Resistance is the opposition of a conductor to current. A good conductor has a low resistance and a poor conductor has a high

RESISTANCE

Figure 25 A hairdryer and a toaster use the heating effect of an electric current

resistance. Copper wire is a good conductor and a current passes through it easily. However, a similar piece of nichrome wire is not so good and less current flows for the same PD – the nichrome wire has more resistance than the copper.

Resistance and the heating effect

Whenever a current flows through a resistance, there is a heating effect. This occurs because as electrons pass through the conductor they collide with the atoms. The electrons may lose energy and the atoms gain energy and vibrate faster. Faster vibrations mean a higher temperature. This heating effect is put to good use in devices such as hairdryers and toasters, which contain heating elements usually made from nichrome wire.

Types of resistive components

Resistors are specially made to provide resistance. In simple circuits they are used to limit the size of current flowing through various components.

The unit of resistance is the **ohm** (Ω). Resistors can have values ranging from a few ohms to several million ohms. The following units are used: 1 kilohm (kΩ) = 1000 Ω; 1 megohm = 1 000 000 Ω.

There are several types of resistors:

* **Variable resistors** (also known as **rheostats**) are used for controlling and varying current. The variable resistor shown in Figure 26 is used to control the current through a bulb, which in turn controls the brightness of the bulb. In radios and hi-fis, variable resistors such as this are used as volume controls.

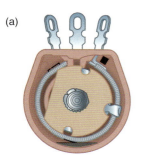

(a)

Figure 26 A variable resistor

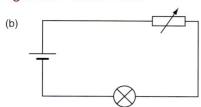

(b)

Figure 27 A variable resistor used to control the brightness of a lamp

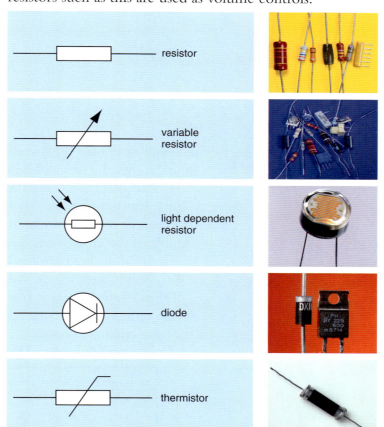

Figure 28 Circuit symbols for the components shown

121

Questions

14 Draw circuit symbols for:
   a) a resistor
   b) a variable resistor.
15 a) What does 'LDR' stand for?
   b) Draw its circuit symbol.
   c) What happens to the resistance of an LDR when light is shone on it?

* **Light-dependent resistors** (LDRs) have a high resistance in the dark but a low resistance in bright conditions. They are used in electronic circuits that switch lights on and off automatically.

* **Diodes** have an extremely high resistance in one direction but a low resistance in the other. In effect, they allow current to flow in one direction only. They are sometimes referred to as rectifiers when they are used to convert alternating current into direct current.

Measuring resistance

To measure the resistance of a component, we pass various currents through it and measure the corresponding voltages across it. This is referred to as the ammeter–voltmeter method. The reason for this is clearly seen in Figure 29.

The variable resistor is used to control the size of the current through the component under test. The ammeter measures the current through the component while the voltmeter measures the voltage across the component.

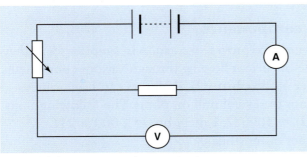

Figure 29 An ammeter–voltmeter circuit

Table 2 shows that the ratio of each pair of readings of potential difference and current has a constant value (4).

Current in A	Potential difference in V	Ratio of potential difference to current in Ω
0.00	0	—
0.25	1	4
0.50	2	4
0.75	3	4
1.00	4	4

Table 2

A graph of PD (in volts) versus current (in amps) shows a straight line through the origin. The slope of the graph is 4.

The constant is the **resistance** of the component measured in ohms. Another way of analysing the results in Table 2 is to say that the current is proportional to the voltage – that is, the current doubles if the voltage doubles.

The relationship between PD and current was first investigated by Georg Ohm, after whom the unit for resistance was named.

Ohm's law states that the current through a wire is proportional to the potential difference across it, provided that the temperature of the wire remains constant.

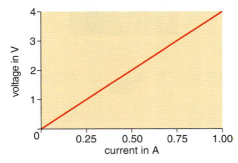

Figure 30

The current, voltage and the resistance of a conductor are related by:

$$\text{voltage} = \text{current} \times \text{resistance}$$
$$(V) \qquad (A) \qquad (\Omega)$$
$$V = I \times R$$

RESISTANCE

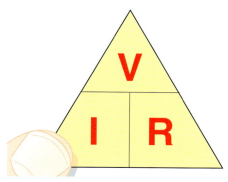

This triangle helps to 'change the subject' in Ohm's law. To find the equation for I, put your thumb over it and it is clear that

$I = \dfrac{V}{R}$

Similarly to find R, put your thumb over it and it is clear that

$R = \dfrac{V}{I}$

Figure 31 Remembering Ohm's law

Examples

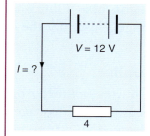

Answer
$V = 12\,V; \quad R = 4\,\Omega; \quad I = ?$

Current $\quad I = \dfrac{V}{R}$

$= \dfrac{12}{4}$

$= \mathbf{3\,A}$

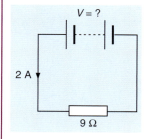

Answer
$I = 2\,A; \quad R = 9\,\Omega; \quad V = ?$

Voltage $\quad V = I \times R$

$= 2 \times 9$

$= \mathbf{18\,V}$

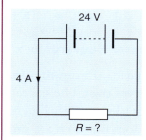

Answer
$V = 24\,V; \quad I = 4\,A; \quad R = ?$

Resistance $\quad R = \dfrac{V}{I}$

$= \dfrac{24}{4}$

$= \mathbf{6\,\Omega}$

Questions

16 Calculate the current flowing through a 10 Ω resistor which has a PD of 20V across it.

17 Calculate the size of a resistor that has a PD of 15V across it, as a consequence of a current of 3A flowing through it.

18 A current of 2A flows through a 25 Ω resistor. Find the PD across the resistor.

19 A PD of 15V is needed to make a current of 2.5A flow through a wire.
   a) What is the resistance of the wire?
   b) What PD is needed to make a current of 2.0A flow through the wire?

20 There is a PD of 6.0V across the ends of a wire of resistance 12 Ω.
   a) What is the current in the wire?
   b) What PD is needed to make a current of 1.5A flow through it?

21 A resistor has a PD of 6V applied across it and the current flowing through is 100 mA. What is the resistance of the resistor?

ELECTRICITY

▶ Current–voltage graphs

Metal conductors obey Ohm's law, provided that their temperature does not change. This is not the case with other types of conductor.

Filament bulb

Using the ammeter–voltmeter method, it is possible to investigate the variation of current with voltage for a filament bulb. Figure 32 shows the results obtained for a filament lamp.

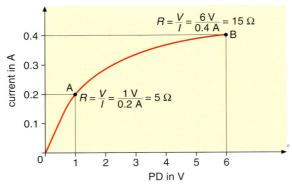

Figure 32 A current–voltage graph for a filament bulb

The graph starts off from the origin a roughly straight line, but it gradually curves over. The current passing through the filament causes it to get hot and this increases its resistance. The result is that the current does not increase proportionately, as it would do if its temperature remained constant. We say that the filament lamp behaves non-ohmically. The calculations on the graph show how the resistance changes.

Diodes

It is clear from the current–voltage graph for a semiconducting diode (Figure 33) that Ohm's law is not obeyed – the current is not proportional to the voltage.

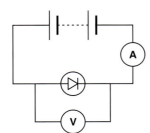

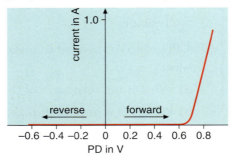

Figure 33 A current–voltage graph for a semiconductor diode

In forward bias (voltage), the current does not begin to flow until the voltage reaches 0.6 V. Then the current increases dramatically. When the polarity of the voltage supply is reversed, virtually no current flows. In other words, the diode is a unidirectional current carrier. It blocks current flow when it is in reverse bias.

CALCULATING THE RESISTANCE OF CIRCUITS

> **Questions**
>
> 22 The results in the table were obtained during the investigation of a filament bulb using the ammeter–voltmeter method.
>
> | Current in mA | 4.219 | 27.7 | 36.1 | 43.7 | 50.6 | 56.9 | 63 | 69 | 74 | 78.6 | 82.3 | 82.3 |
> |---|---|---|---|---|---|---|---|---|---|---|---|---|
> | Voltage in V | 0.43 | 0.69 | 1.49 | 2.32 | 3.17 | 4.04 | 4.92 | 5.81 | 6.7 | 7.56 | 8.42 | 9.3 |
>
> a) Plot a graph of voltage on the y-axis against current on the x-axis, using the following scales:
>   y-axis: 2 cm = 1 V
>   x-axis: 2 cm = 10 mA
> b) Draw a smooth curve through the points. Does the bulb obey Ohm's law?
> c) Explain why the graph of voltage against current is a curve.
>
> 23 The table below shows the readings obtained while investigating the behaviour of a diode.
>
> | Voltage in V | 0 | 0.1 | 0.2 | 0.3 | 0.4 | 0.5 | 0.6 | 0.7 |
> |---|---|---|---|---|---|---|---|---|
> | Current in mA | 0 | 0.1 | 0.1 | 0.1 | 0.1 | 1.5 | 73 | 250 |
> | Resistance in Ω | | | | | | | | |
>
> a) Draw a graph of current versus voltage.
> b) Does the diode obey Ohm's law?
> c) Copy and complete the table.

Summary of units used in the study of electricity

There are a bewildering number of physical quantities, units and symbols used in the study of electricity. Table 3 gives a summary.

Name of quantity	Symbol	Unit	Symbol for unit
Charge	Q	coulomb	C
Current	I	ampere	A
Resistance	R	ohm	Ω
Voltage	V	volt	V
Potential difference	PD	volt	V
Electromotive force	EMF	volt	V

Table 3

Calculating the resistance of circuits

Series circuits

The total resistance of two or more resistors in series is simply the sum of the individual resistances of the resistors:

$$R_{total} = R_1 + R_2 + R_3$$

In Figure 34, the three resistors could be replaced by a single resistor of $(4 + 8 + 6 =)$ 18 Ω.

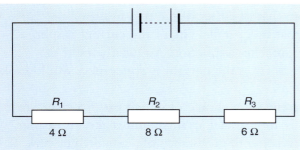

Figure 34 Calculating the total resistance of three resistors in a series circuit

Parallel circuits

The formula for calculating the combined resistance of three resistors in parallel is:

$$\frac{1}{R_{total}} = \frac{1}{R_1} + \frac{1}{R_2} + \frac{1}{R_3}$$

When considering two resistors in parallel, this formula can be shortened to:

$$R_{total} = \frac{R_1 \times R_2}{R_1 + R_2}$$

$$= \frac{\text{product}}{\text{sum}}$$

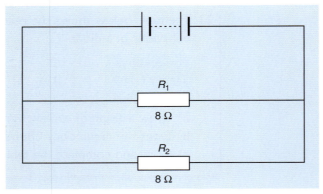

Figure 35 Calculating the total resistance of two resistors in a parallel circuit

> **Example**
> Find the combined resistance of two 8 Ω resistors in parallel.
>
> **Answer**
> $$R_{total} = \frac{\text{product}}{\text{sum}}$$
> $$= \frac{8 \times 8}{8 + 8}$$
> $$= \frac{64}{16}$$
> $$= 4\,\Omega$$

This appears to be a surprising result. How can the combined resistance be smaller than that of either of the two resistors?

Recall that in a parallel circuit the current is split when it approaches a junction. An enlargement of junction A, as far as the current is concerned, would look like Figure 36.

The current has a choice of which path to take – in other words, the parallel arrangement makes life 'easier' for the current, so the resistance of a parallel network of resistors is always smaller than the value of the smallest resistor.

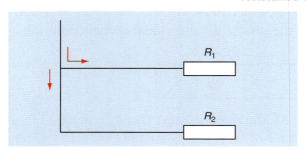

Figure 36

CALCULATING THE RESISTANCE OF CIRCUITS

Questions

24 Calculate the combined resistance in each of the following combinations of resistors:

a)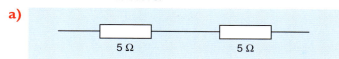

b)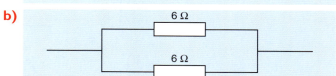

c)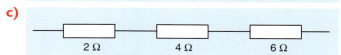

d)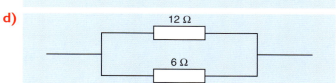

e)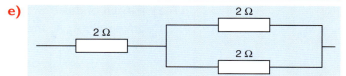

f)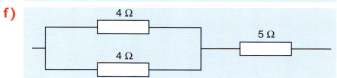

g)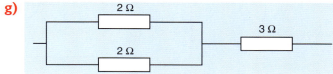

h)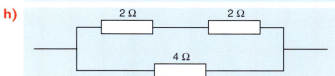

i)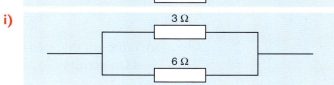

j)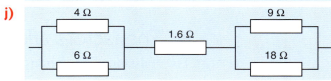

25 If you are provided with three resistors of 1 Ω, 2 Ω and 3 Ω, what different values of resistance can you get by making up different series and parallel circuits?

26 a) Calculate the value of the current from the cell in each of these circuits:

i)
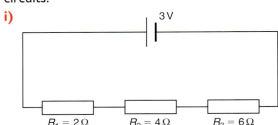

ii)
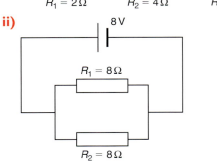

b) What is the voltage drop across each $8\,\Omega$ resistor?

27 a) In each of these circuits, calculate the current shown by ammeters A_1, A_2 and A_3.

i)
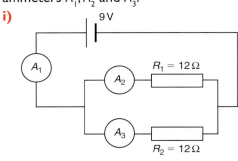

ii)
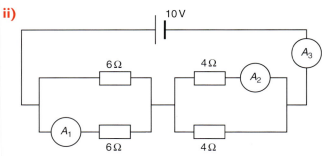

b) What are the voltage drops across each $6\,\Omega$ resistor and each $4\,\Omega$ resistor?

▶ The factors affecting resistance

The resistance of a conductor depends on several factors:

* *Length* – increasing the length of a wire increases its resistance.
* *Cross-sectional area* – increasing the thickness of a wire decreases its resistance. Conversely, decreasing the thickness of a wire increases its resistance.

* *Material* – a nichrome wire has more resistance than a copper wire with the same dimensions.
* *Temperature* – for metal conductors, resistance increases with temperature. For semiconductors, it decreases with temperature.

Investigating how the resistance of a metallic conductor at constant temperature depends on length

1. Measure and cut off one metre of nichrome resistance wire.
2. Attach it with Sellotape to a meter ruler – make sure there are no kinks in the wire.
3. Measure and record the current through and the voltage across 40 cm of the nichrome wire as shown in Figure 37. Use Ohm's law to calculate its resistance.
4. Repeat this process for increasing lengths of the wire up to 1.0 m.
5. Be careful to switch off the current between measurements to ensure that the temperature of the wire does not increase.
6. Draw a graph with resistance on the *y*-axis and length on the *x*-axis.
7. Draw a line of best fit through the points.

It should be clear from the graph that the resistance of the wire is directly proportional to its length.

Investigating how the resistance of a metallic conductor at constant temperature depends on the cross-sectional area

The controlled variables in this investigation are length and type of metal. Assuming that all the wires used have a uniform cross-sectional area, then measuring the diameter (*D*) will allow the cross-sectional area to be calculated.

1. You can use a micrometer screw gauge to measure the diameter or, more simply, measure the length (*l*) of 20 turns of the wire wound tightly together on a wooden dowel. Divide this length by 20 to calculate its diameter:

$$D = \frac{l}{20}$$

$$\text{cross-sectional area} = \frac{\pi D^2}{4}$$

2. Repeat this process for five further thicknesses of the same length of wire and same type of material.
3. For each thickness, measure and record the current through it and the voltage across it.
4. As before use Ohm's law to determine the resistance for that thickness.
5. Record your results in a table as shown below.

Cross-sectional area in mm²	Current in A	Voltage in V	Resistance in Ω	1/cross-sectional area in mm²

ELECTRICITY

A graph of resistance (*y*-axis) versus the reciprocal of the cross-sectional area (*x*-axis) should give a straight line through the origin – implying that the resistance of a wire is inversely proportional to its cross-sectional area.

Investigating how the resistance of a metallic conductor at constant temperature depends on the material it is made from

The controlled variables in this investigation are the length and the thickness of wire. It is reasonable to expect that the resistance should depend on the type of material from which a wire is made.

Using one metre of 32 swg copper wire, measure and record the resistance as before. Then repeat the process using the same dimensions of wires such as nichrome and constantan.

▶ Electrical energy

If 1 coulomb of charge gains or loses 1 joule of energy between two points, there is a potential difference of 1 volt between those two points.

$$PD = \frac{\text{energy transferred}}{\text{charge}}$$

Rearranging this formula gives us:

energy transferred = PD × charge

It is much easier to measure current than charge, because:

charge = current × time

Substituting for charge gives a very useful formula for energy transferred in an electric circuit:

energy transferred = PD × current × time
$$= V \times I \times t$$

Example
If 0.5 A flows through a bulb connected across a 6 V power supply for 10 seconds, how much energy is transferred?

Answer

Energy = $V \times I \times t$
    = 6 × 0.5 × 10
    = 30 J

So the rate of energy transfer must be 30 J in 10 s, and that is 3 J per second, or 3 watts.

⇒ DID YOU KNOW?
In 1995, the Norwegians topped the league as the biggest consumers of electrical energy per capita. Twice as much as the average American!

Questions

28 How much electrical energy does a 1000W convector heater consume in 1 hour?

29 In 10 seconds, an electric toaster consumes 15 000 joules of energy from the mains supply. What is its power:
  a) in watts
  b) in kilowatts?

30 A study lamp draws a current of 0.25A at 230V from the mains supply. Calculate the amount of energy it consumes in 60 seconds.

31 a) The starter motor of a car has a power rating of 960W. If it is switched on for 5 seconds, how much energy does it use?
  b) The same starter motor is powered by connecting it to a 12V car battery. How much current does it use?

▶ Electrical power

In Chapter 3, you learned that the formula for mechanical power of a machine is defined as the rate at which energy is transformed and is given by:

$$\text{power} = \frac{\text{energy transformed}}{\text{time}}$$

We have seen that in an electrical circuit:

$$\text{energy transformed} = \text{potential difference} \times \text{current} \times \text{time}$$

Substituting for energy transformed:

$$\text{power} = \frac{\text{potential difference} \times \text{current} \times \text{time}}{\text{time}}$$

or

$$\begin{array}{cccc}\text{electrical power} = & \text{potential difference} & \times & \text{current} \\ (\text{W}) & (\text{V}) & & (\text{A})\end{array}$$

⇨ DID YOU KNOW?

A single lightning strike is made up of six million volts with a peak current of 20 000 amps. This corresponds to an electrical power of 12 TW (12 000 000 000 000 W) – many times greater than the average coal-fired power station!

Example

A study lamp is rated at 60W, 230V. How much current is the bulb carrying?

Answer

$$\text{power} = V \times I$$
$$60 = 240 \times I$$
$$I = \frac{60}{240}$$
$$= 0.25\,\text{A}$$

Domestic appliances such as toasters, hairdryers and TVs have a power rating marked on them in watts or in kilowatts (1 kW = 1000 W).

Some typical power ratings are shown in Figure 37. Each number tells you the power the appliance will take when connected to a 230V supply.

1100W   2200W   60W

Figure 37 The typical power ratings of some household appliances

Because power = $V \times I$ and Ohm's law is $V = I \times R$

So power = I^2R

$= \dfrac{V^2}{R}$

These two alternative formulae give the electrical power dissipated (converted) into heat in resistors and heating elements. The heat dissipated is sometimes referred to as 'ohmic losses'.

Example
What power is dissipated in a 10 Ω resistor when the current through it is:

a) 2A **b)** 4A?

Answer

a) power = I^2R
$= 2^2 \times 10$
= 40 W

b) power = I^2R
$= 4^2 \times 10$
= 160 W

This example shows that when the current is doubled, the power dissipated is quadrupled! This idea has important implications for electricity transmission (Chapter 7).

ELECTRICITY IN THE HOME

Questions

32 If an electric heater takes a current of 4A when connected to a 230V supply, what is its power?

33 If a light bulb has a power of 48W when connected to a 12V supply, what is the current through it?

34 Copy and complete the table for domestic appliances, all of which operate at 230V.

Name of appliance	Power rating	Current drawn	Resistance
Bulb of study lamp	60 W		
Television	80 W		
Toaster	1200 W		
Convector heater	2 kW		
Shower	3 kW		

35 An electric kettle has an element of resistance 48 Ω. Calculate how much power it uses when it is connected to the 240V mains supply.

▶ Electricity in the home

Alternating current and direct current

A direct current (d.c.) always flows in the same direction, from a fixed positive terminal to the fixed negative terminal of a supply. A typical d.c. circuit is shown in Figure 38a. A cell or battery gives a constant (steady) direct current. A graph of voltage versus time for a d.c. supply is shown in Figure 38b. The current is described as being unidirectional.

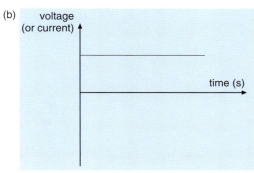

Figure 38

The electricity supply to your home is an alternating current (a.c.) supply. In an a.c. supply, the voltage (and hence the current) change size and direction in a regular and repetitive way (Figure 39). In fact, the mains voltage changes from $+325$V to -325V. The average value of this voltage is 230V. The current changes direction 100 times every second and makes 50 complete cycles per second – hence the frequency of the mains is 50 Hz.

It is clear from Figure 39 why an a.c. supply is said to be bidirectional.

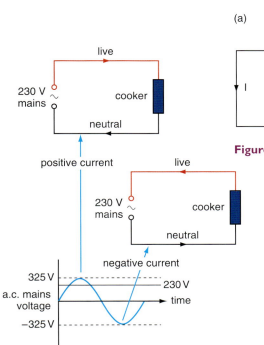

Figure 39

Two-way switches

In most two-storey houses, you can turn the landing lights on or off from upstairs or downstairs. Two-way switches are used for this.

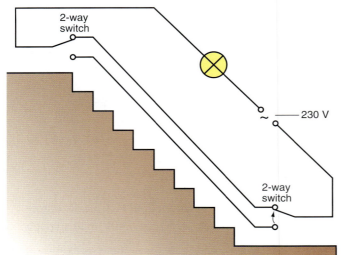

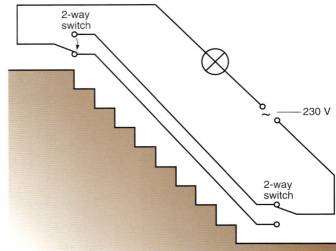

Figure 40a Going to bed at night, when both switches are up, the circuit is complete and a current flows through the bulb

Figure 40b At the top of the stairs, one of the switches is pressed down and the circuit is broken. You should verify for yourself what happens when the person comes downstairs. The effect is that each switch reverses the effect of the other one

Electrical safety

Voltages of 50V and currents as low as 50 mA can be fatal so electrical safety is vitally important.

The three-pin plug

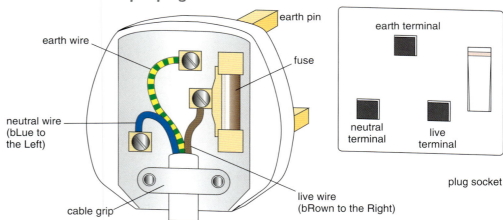

Figure 41 A correctly wired three-pin plug

Wiring a three-pin plug

* Fix the 3-core cable tightly with the cord grip.
* The wire with the blue insulation is the neutral wire – connect this to the left-hand pin.
* The brown insulated wire is the live wire – connect this to the right-hand pin. This pin has the fuse attached because it is connected to the live wire.

ELECTRICITY IN THE HOME

* The wire with the yellow and green insulation is the earth wire – connect this to the top pin.
* Each of these wires should be wrapped around its securing screw so that it is tightened as the screw tightens.

Each pin in the plug fits into a corresponding hole in the socket. The earth pin is longer than the others so that it goes into the socket first and pushes aside safety covers, which cover the rear of the neutral and live holes in the socket.

If an appliance becomes live, a current flows through the earth wire and then from the socket earth connection to the earth via a water pipe. During the process, the fuse in the plug will blow. Before it is replaced, the appliance should be checked by a qualified electrician.

Fuses

A **fuse** is a device which is meant to prevent damage to an appliance. Those used are either a 3 A (red) fuse for appliances up to 720 W or 13 A (brown) fuse for appliances between 720 W and 3 kW. If a larger-than-usual current flows, the fuse will melt and so break the circuit.

Figure 42 Fuses

Selecting a fuse

Every appliance has a power rating. How much current the appliance will use is found using the power formula:

$$\text{power} = \text{voltage} \times \text{current}$$

For example, the jig-saw shown in Figure 44 has a power of 350 W. So the current it draws when connected to the mains is given by:

$$\text{current} = \frac{\text{power}}{\text{voltage}}$$
$$= \frac{350}{240}$$
$$= 1.46 \, \text{A}$$

Figure 43 The power rating label on the side of an electric jig-saw

This is the normal current the device uses – any large current can destroy it. A 3 A fuse would allow a normal working current to flow and protect the jig-saw from larger currents. A 13 A fuse would allow a dangerously high current to flow and still not 'blow'. So it is important to use the correct size of fuse. It is important to remember that a fuse does not protect the person using the appliance. It can take 1 to 2 seconds for a fuse to melt – enough time for the user to receive a fatal electric shock.

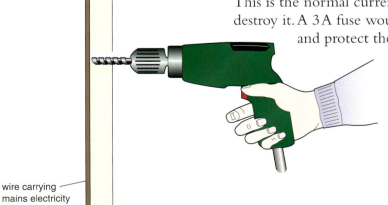

wire carrying mains electricity

Figure 44 If there is no earth wire connected to the casing of the drill, the current will flow through the person

The earth wire

An **earth** link prevents damage to the user. Suppose a fault develops in an electric fire and the element is in contact with the casing of the fire. The casing will be live and if someone were to touch it they would get a possibly fatal electric shock as the current rushes through their body to earth. The earth wire prevents this – it offers a low resistance route of escape, enabling the current to go to earth by a wire rather than through a human body. After a few seconds, the large current will blow the fuse. Any appliance with a metal casing could become live if a fault developed.

Double insulation

Appliances such as vacuum cleaners and hairdryers are usually **double insulated**. The appliance is encased in an insulating plastic case and is connected to the supply by a two-core insulated cable containing only a live and a neutral wire. Any metal attachments that a user might touch are fitted into the plastic case so that they do not make a direct connection with the motor or other internal electrical parts. The symbol for double insulated appliances is:

Paying for electricity

Electricity companies bill customers for electrical energy in units known as **kilowatt-hours** (kWh). These are sometimes called 'Units' of electricity. One kilowatt-hour is the amount of energy transferred when 1000 W is delivered for 1 hour. You should prove to yourself that

$$1 \text{ kWh} = 3\,600\,000 \text{ joules}.$$

There are two important numbers on an electricity bill:

Northern Electricity Board				Customer account no: 3427 364
Present meter reading	Previous meter reading	Units used	Cost per unit (incl. VAT)	£
57139	55652	1487	11.0p	163.57

The difference between the present reading and the previous reading is the number of Units used. In this particular example:

$$57139 - 55652 = 1487 \text{ Units (kWh)}$$

1487 Units have been used. If the cost of a Unit is known, then the cost of the electricity used can be determined.

Different appliances have different power ratings and the following two formulae are very useful in calculating the cost of using a particular appliance for a given amount of time:

number of Units used = power rating (in kilowatts) × time (in hours)

total cost = number of Units used × cost per Unit

> *Example*
>
> 1. Calculate the cost of using a 100 W study lamp for 8 hours (assume that the price of a Unit is 12p).
>
> **Answer**
>
> power = 100 W = 0.1 kW
>
> time = 8 hours
>
> number of Units used = 0.1 × 8
> = 0.8
>
> cost = 0.8 × 12
> = **9.6p**
>
> 2. Calculate the cost of using a 3 kW immersion heater for 8 hours.
>
> **Answer**
>
> power = 3.0 kW
>
> time = 8 hours
>
> number of Units used = 3.0 × 8
> = 24 units
>
> cost = 24 × 12
> = **£2.88**
>
> Clearly, studying is much cheaper than having a bath!

Questions

36 a) What are the colours of:
  i) the live
  ii) the neutral
  iii) the earth wire?

b) The earth wire comes loose in a convection heater, and a wire from the heating element touches the metal case.
  i) What will happen to a person who touches the case when the heater is turned on?
  ii) If the earth wire had remained in its correct position, how would it and the fuse (in the plug) have worked together to make the heater safe?

37 Explain what is meant by:

a) a direct current   **b)** an alternating current.

Draw sketch graphs to illustrate your answer.

38 Circuit breakers are often used instead of fuses, especially with appliances that require a large current to make them work. Why are circuit breakers better than fuses in these cases?

39 A bedside lamp is rated at 230V, 60W.
   a) Calculate the current that will flow when the lamp is in use.
   b) Why would it be safe to use a 3A fuse in the plug?

40 Cartridge fuses are normally available as 3A, 5A or 13A.
   a) What would probably happen if you used a 3A fuse in the plug for a 3 kW electric fire?
   b) Why is it bad practice to use a 13A fuse in a plug for a 60W study lamp?
   c) What size of fuse would you use for a hairdryer labelled 240V, 800W? Explain how you worked out your answer.

41 What is the highest number of 60W bulbs that can be run off the 230V mains if you are not going to overload a 5A fuse?

42 A 13A socket is designed to allow a current of 13A to be drawn safely from it. Mr White connected the following appliances to a single 13A socket using a 4-way extension lead:

   a 2.4 kW electric kettle; a 3 kW washing machine;
   an 800W television; a 1300W toaster.

   a) Calculate the current through each appliance, assuming that the supply voltage is 230V.
   b) Assuming that the plug from the extension lead contained a 13A fuse, what would happen if he attempted to use all the appliances at the same time?

43 Calculate how much electrical energy, in kWh, is used for:
   a) a 100W lamp on for 12 hours
   b) a 250W television on for 4 hours
   c) a 2400W kettle on for 5 minutes?

44 If the price for 1 Unit is 12p, what is the running cost of each item in question **43**?

45 An electric shower is rated at 230V, 15A.
   a) Calculate the electrical power used by the shower heater.
   b) Calculate the cost of a 10-minute shower if 1 kWh costs 12p.

Search
▶ lightning
▶ current electricity
▶ diodes
▶ static electricity
▶ domestic electricity

Exam questions

1 a) Large amounts of electric charge can collect on clouds. What danger can this cause for tall buildings beneath the clouds? *(2 marks)*

b) i) Explain how a balloon can become positively charged when it is rubbed with a cloth. *(3 marks)*

ii) A second balloon is rubbed with another cloth and is hung beside the first. The diagram below shows how the two balloons hang side by side.

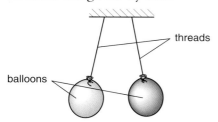

What can you tell about the charges on the balloons? Explain your answer. *(4 marks)*

c) i) Draw an electric circuit diagram in which two bulbs are connected in parallel and are controlled by a single switch. *(3 marks)*

ii) The light bulbs get dimmer. What can you tell about the current flowing in the bulbs? *(1 mark)*

d) i) Show that the total resistance between R and T in the circuit below is 10 Ω. *(4 marks)*

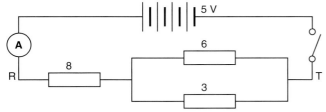

ii) Calculate the reading on the ammeter when the switch is closed. Show clearly how you get your answer. *(3 marks)*

iii) Calculate the voltage across the 8 Ω resistor. Show clearly how you get your answer. *(3 marks)*

iv) Calculate the power in the 8 Ω resistor. Show clearly how you get your answer. *(4 marks)*

v) What is the voltage across the 6 Ω resistor? Show clearly how you get your answer. *(2 marks)*

vi) What is the voltage across the 3 Ω resistor? *(1 mark)*

2 a) Two identical lamps are to be connected in parallel to a battery.

i) Draw the circuit diagram to show how the lamps would be connected. *(2 marks)*

ii) The resistance of one lamp is 0.6 Ω and the resistance of the other is 0.3 Ω. What is the total resistance of the lamps in parallel? Show clearly how you get your answer. *(3 marks)*

iii) Both lamps are shining brightly. Then one lamp blows and goes out. Would the brightness of the other lamp increase, decrease or stay the same? Give a reason for your answer. *(2 marks)*

b) A student is investigating how the current passing through a resistance wire depends on the voltage across its ends. The circuit diagram below shows part of the circuit which she set up.

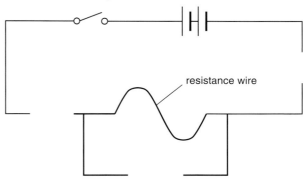

i) Copy the diagram and, in the correct space, draw the correct symbol for the apparatus she would use:
- to measure the current in the circuit
- to measure the voltage across the wire
- to change the current flowing in the resistance wire. *(3 marks)*

The student obtains the following set of results:

Voltage in V	0	0.2	0.4	0.6	0.8	1.0
Current in mA	0	25	50	70	100	125

ii) On graph paper, using the axes shown on the following page, plot a graph of voltage against current and draw the best fit line. *(4 marks)*

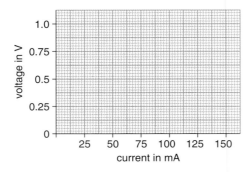

iii) In the table on the previous page, which current was recorded incorrectly by the student? *(1 mark)*

iv) Calculate the resistance of this wire when the current flowing in it is 50 mA. *(4 marks)*

v) Is the resistance of this wire constant for currents up to 50 mA? Give a reason for your answer. *(2 marks)*

vi) Before reading the meter, the student switched the apparatus off for a few minutes. Then she switched the apparatus on again, and read the ammeter and voltmeter. Give a reason, not concerned with cost or safety, why she might have done this. *(1 mark)*

3 a) The diagram below shows a 1.5V cell connected to two *identical* bulbs and a switch. When the switch is closed, both bulbs light.

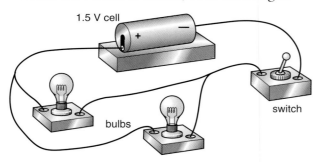

i) Draw the circuit diagram for this arrangement using standard symbols. *(4 marks)*

ii) What name is given to this type of circuit? *(1 mark)*

iii) Describe and explain what you would observe if one of the bulbs were removed and the switch closed. *(2 marks)*

When both bulbs are lit, the current passing through one of them is 0.3 A.

iv) Calculate the resistance of this bulb. Show clearly how you get your answer. *(4 marks)*

b) Another circuit is made using one of the bulbs and two 1.5V cells as shown below.

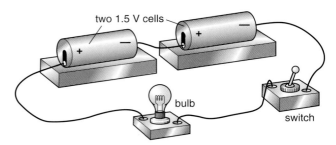

i) What is the voltage across the bulb? *(2 marks)*

ii) Calculate the current that passes through this circuit when the switch is closed. Show clearly how you get your answer. *(4 marks)*

iii) Using your answers to part **b) ii)** and the current passing through the bulb in part **a)**, comment on the brightness of the bulb in the circuit above. *(2 marks)*

c) The diagram below shows the main parts of the fuel gauge of a car. The slider completes the circuit so that the ammeter shows a current. As the level of fuel falls, the float also falls and the slider moves to the left, keeping contact with the resistance wire.

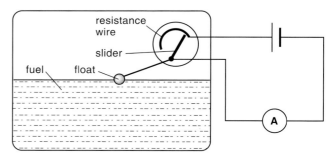

i) As the slider moves to the left (anticlockwise) how does the resistance of the circuit change? Explain your answer. *(2 marks)*

ii) How does the current in the ammeter change as the fuel level falls? Explain your answer. *(2 marks)*

4 a) Mary needs to measure the electrical resistance of a filament light bulb.
  i) Draw a diagram of the circuit that she would use to get a series of voltage and current readings from which to find a series of values of the bulb's resistance. *(2 marks)*

Below is a table of the readings that she obtained in her experiment.

Current in A	0	0.10	0.20	0.30	0.40	0.50
Voltage in V	0	0.5	1.0	1.8	3.2	5.0

  ii) Calculate the resistance of the filament of the bulb when the current has a value of 0.1 A and when the current has a value of 0.4 A. *(3 marks)*
  iii) Plot a graph of voltage (*y*-axis) against current (*x*-axis). *(2 marks)*
  iv) Explain the shape of the graph. *(2 marks)*

b) An electric fire is connected to the mains supply by means of a three-pin plug.
  i) The electric fire has a rating of 2000 W when used on a 230 V mains supply. Calculate the rating of the fuse suitable for use with this fire. The available fuse ratings are 1 A, 3 A, 5 A and 13 A. *(4 marks)*
  ii) Describe the size of the current in the live, neutral and earth wires when the fire is switched on and working properly. *(1 mark)*
  iii) The live wire becomes loose and comes in contact with the metal body of the electric fire. Describe the danger that could arise when the electric fire is switched on. *(1 mark)*
  iv) How should the earth wire be connected so as to remove this danger? *(1 mark)*
  v) How should the fuse be connected so as to remove this danger? *(1 mark)*
  vi) Explain how the action of the earth wire and the fuse remove this danger. *(1 mark)*

5 a) Mrs Johnston's electricity meter was read at 1 month intervals.
  Reading at 1 April 2000   11 897 kWh
  Reading at 1 May 2000   12 107 kWh
  i) How many Units of electricity were used in the Johnston home during April? *(1 mark)*

  ii) If 1 Unit of electricity costs 12p, calculate the cost of electricity to Mrs Johnston during April. Show clearly how you get your answer. *(2 marks)*

b) An electric fire is wired using a three-pin plug as shown in the diagram below.

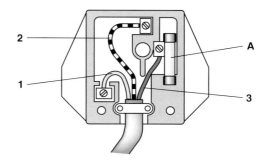

  i) Name the part labelled A. *(1 mark)*
  ii) Which of the wires 1, 2 or 3 should be connected to the metal casing of the fire? *(1 mark)*
  iii) State the colours of the insulation on wires 1 and 2. *(2 marks)*

c) i) Two copper wires have the same length but different thicknesses. How does the resistance of a wire change as its thickness increases? *(2 marks)*
  ii) Two copper wires have the same thickness but different lengths. How does the resistance of a wire change as its length increases? *(2 marks)*

d) i) Copy the circuit diagram below and complete the two-way switches A and B so that the bulb lights. *(2 marks)*

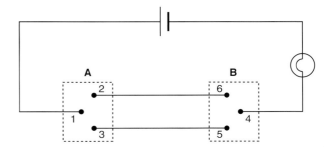

ii) Now that you have completed the switches, describe the path of the current from the positive terminal of the battery to the negative terminal, by copying and completing the following sentence.
The current flows from the positive terminal to 1 to ___ to ___ to ___ to the lamp and to the negative terminal.
(2 marks)

e) Kevin set up the circuit shown below using two identical resistors.

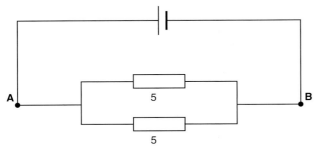

i) How are the resistors said to be connected? *(1 mark)*

ii) What is the total resistance between A and B? *(2 marks)*

iii) Copy the circuit diagram and mark, with an X, the position where an ammeter should be connected to measure the current through one resistor only. *(1 mark)*

6 a) A television set is marked 230 V, 80 W.
i) Explain carefully what these numbers mean. *(2 marks)*
ii) Calculate the current that passes through the television when it is on. Show clearly how you get your answer. *(3 marks)*
iii) Select a fuse that should be fitted to this appliance from the list below. Explain your choice. *(2 marks)*
1 A, 3 A, 5 A, 13 A
iv) Calculate the resistance of the television set. Show clearly how you get your answer. *(3 marks)*

v) The flex that connects this television to the mains has only two wires inside it. The diagram below shows the inside of a three-pin plug. Copy the diagram and complete it to show how the plug should be wired. Label each wire with its name and colour. *(3 marks)*

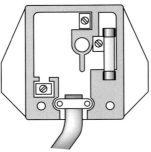

vi) To which of these wires should the switch on the television be connected? *(1 mark)*

vii) Apart from allowing the user to switch the television on and off, this is done for another reason. What is this other reason? *(1 mark)*

viii) Explain how the owner of this television is protected from possible electric shock. *(3 marks)*

b) The oven of an electric cooker is rated at 8 kW.
i) Calculate the cost of using the oven to cook for 2 hours. The cost of electricity is 12p per unit. Show clearly how you get your answer. *(3 marks)*
ii) A copper cable of length 5 m and cross-sectional area 2 mm^2 has a resistance of 0.045 Ω. The copper cable used to connect the cooker to the mains supply is 15 m long and has a cross-sectional area of 6 mm^2. Calculate the resistance of the cable. Show clearly how you get your answer. *(6 marks)*
iii) When the oven is on, the same current passes through the cable as the heating elements. Explain why the cable does not heat up. *(2 marks)*

7 Electromagnetism

▶ Properties of magnets

A **magnet** has the property of attracting iron and steel, and to a much lesser extent cobalt and nickel. These substances are known as ferromagnetic materials. All other substances are, for practical purposes, non-magnetic.

When a magnet is dipped into iron filings, it is clear that most filings cling to the ends of the magnet and very few to the middle (Figure 1). The attraction is greatest at the ends, which are called **poles**. Ancient mariners knew that when magnets are suspended so that they can rotate freely, they always settle down pointing in the same direction, approximately north–south. The same end always swings round to the north and this is called the north-seeking pole, or simply the north pole. The other end is the south-seeking pole or south pole, see Figure 2.

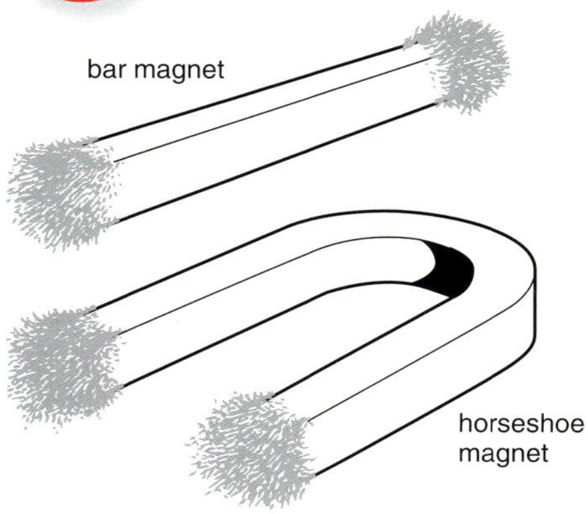

Figure 1

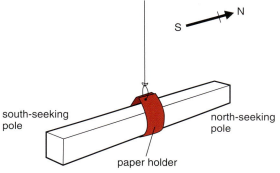

Figure 2 Magnets have poles

Experiments with different poles (Figure 3) give us a result which is called the first law of magnetism:

> Unlike poles attract; like poles repel.

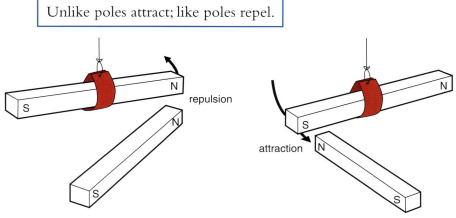

Figure 3 Poles interacting with each other

▶ Current and magnetism

When an electric current flows through a wire, not only does it heat up, but a magnetic field is created around the wire.

143

ELECTROMAGNETISM

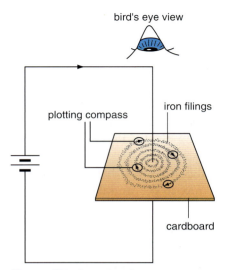

Figure 4 To show that there is a magnetic field around a current-carrying wire

The field due to a current-carrying wire

In Figure 4, a long, straight wire carrying an electrical current is placed vertically through a horizontal piece of cardboard. Iron filings are sprinkled onto the cardboard to reveal the magnetic lines of force when the current is switched on and the cardboard is tapped lightly.

This experiment shows that:

* if the current is large, the lines of force are concentrated, which means that the magnetic field is strong
* the magnetic field gets weaker further away from the wire
* the direction of the magnetic field lines can be found using a plotting compass.

The field due to current-carrying coils

Figure 5 shows the magnetic field around a single loop of wire that is carrying a current. Near A, the field lines point anticlockwise as you look at them, and near B, the lines point clockwise. In the middle, the fields from each part of the loop combine to produce a magnetic field running from left to right.

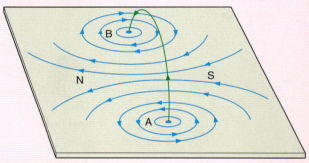

Figure 5 The magnetic field around a single loop of current-carrying wire

This loop of wire is like a very short bar magnet. Magnetic field lines come out of the left-hand side (north pole) and go back into the right-hand side (south pole).

The strength of the magnetic field can be increased by increasing the number of turns of wire in the coil, and also by increasing the current in the coil.

Making a simple electromagnet

A stronger magnetic field can be made by wrapping a wire in the form of a long coil, which is referred to as a **solenoid**.

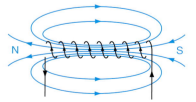 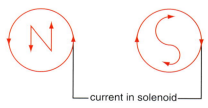

Figure 6 The pattern of magnetic field around a solenoid

Figure 7 This is a good way of working out the polarity of an end of a solenoid

MAGNETIC FORCE ON A CURRENT-CARRYING WIRE – THE MOTOR EFFECT

The strength of the magnetic field produced by a solenoid can be increased by:

* using a larger current
* using more turns of wire
* putting a soft iron rod into the middle of the solenoid.

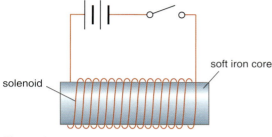

Figure 8 A simple electromagnet

Putting a soft iron rod in the solenoid makes a simple **electromagnet**. Unlike an ordinary magnet, an electromagnet can be switched on and off. In a simple electromagnet, a coil consisting of several hundred turns of insulated copper wire is wound round a core, usually made of iron. When a current flows through the coil, it produces a magnetic field. This magnetises the iron core, producing a magnetic field about a thousand times stronger than that produced by the coil alone.

Soft iron is used because it is easy to magnetise and demagnetise. Electromagnetism is only temporary, and is lost as soon as the current through the coil is switched off. Steel would not be suitable as a core because it would become permanently magnetised.

Advantages of electromagnets compared to magnets

Electromagnets are used in preference to normal magnets because:

* the strength of the electromagnet can be varied
* the magnetism can be switched off and on.

Uses of electromagnets

Electromagnets can be used:

* to separate metallic from non-metallic materials
* to lift magnetic materials like iron and steel in scrapyards
* in relay switches and bells.

Figure 9 Large electromagnets are used in scrapyards to separate magnetic materials from non-magnetic materials

▶ Magnetic force on a current-carrying wire – the motor effect

Figure 10 shows a length of copper wire placed in a magnetic field. The copper wire is not magnetic so the wire itself is not affected by the magnet. However, with a current passing through it, there is a force on the wire. Where does this force come from?

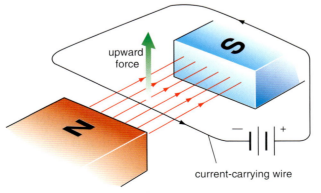

Figure 10 The movement of a current-carrying wire in a magnetic field

The force arises because the current produces its own magnetic field, which interacts with the field of the magnet. The resulting magnetic field is shown in Figure 11. Note how the originally circular field lines due to the current in the wire have become distorted. The field lines below the wire are concentrated but the field lines above the wire are not. The result is that the wire experiences a force as the field lines tend to straighten.

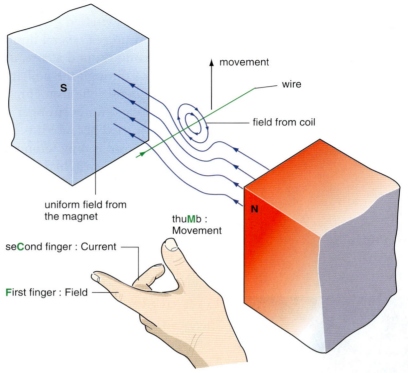

Figure 11 Fleming's left-hand rule

If either the current in the wire changes direction or the polarity of the magnet is reversed, then the direction of the force on the wire is reversed.

The force is increased if:

* the current in the wire is increased
* a stronger magnet is used
* the length of the wire exposed to the magnetic field is increased.

The relationship between the direction of motion, the current and the magnetic field when a current-carrying wire is in a magnetic field is predicted by **Fleming's left-hand rule**. This states that if the thumb and first two fingers of the left hand are held at right angles to each other, then the thu**m**b points in the direction of the force or **m**otion, the **f**irst finger will be pointing in the direction of the **f**ield and the se**c**ond finger will be pointing in the direction of the **c**urrent.

When applying this rule, it is important to remember how the field and current directions are defined:

* The field direction is from the north pole of a magnet to the south pole.
* The current direction is from the positive (+) terminal of a battery round to the negative (−).

MAGNETIC FORCE ON A CURRENT-CARRYING WIRE – THE MOTOR EFFECT

Fleming's left-hand rule only applies if the current and field directions are at right angles to each other. If the current and fields are parallel, there is no force on the wire and it will not move.

Several devices use the fact that there is a force on a current-carrying conductor in a magnetic field. They include the loudspeaker and the electric motor.

The turning effect on a current-carrying coil in a magnetic field

The loop of wire in Figure 12 lies between the poles of a magnet. The current flows in opposite directions along the two sides of the loop. If you apply Fleming's left-hand rule, when a current is passed through the loop, one side of the loop is pushed up and the other side is pushed down. In other words, there is a turning effect on the loop.

If the number of loops is increased to form a coil, the turning effect is greatly increased. This is the principle used in electric motors.

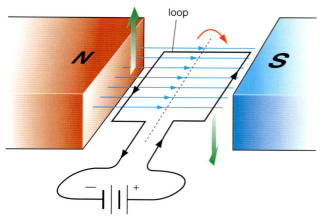

Figure 12 When a current is passed through the loop, it experiences a turning effect

The d.c. electric motor

Figure 13 shows a simple electric motor. It runs on direct current (d.c.), the unidirectional current that flows from a battery.

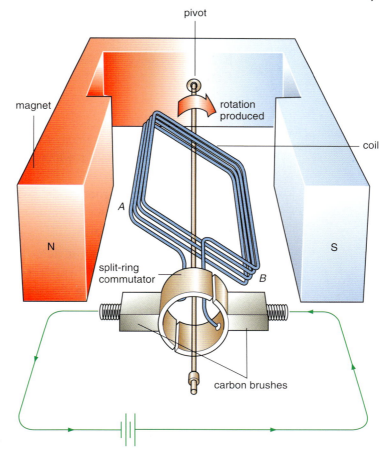

Figure 13 A simple electric motor

ELECTROMAGNETISM

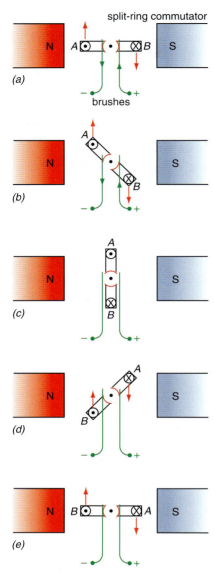

Figure 14 The turning action of the coil in the electric motor

The coil is made of insulated copper wire. The coil is free to rotate on an axle between the poles of a magnet. The commutator, or split-ring, is fixed to the coil and rotates with it. Figure 14 details this action. The brushes are two contacts that rub against the commutator and keep the coil connected to the battery. They are usually made of carbon.

When the coil is horizontal, the forces are furthest apart and have their maximum turning effect on the coil. With no change to the forces, the coil would eventually come to rest in the vertical position. However, as the coil overshoots the vertical, the commutator changes the direction of the current through it. So the forces change direction and push the coil further around until it is again vertical, and so on. In this way the coil keeps rotating clockwise, half a turn at a time. If either the battery or the poles of the magnet are reversed, the coil would rotate anticlockwise.

The turning effect on the coil can be increased by:

* increasing the current in the coil
* increasing the number of turns in the coil
* increasing the strength of the magnetic field
* increasing the area of the coil.

Figure 15 A cut-away view of a De Walt drill, showing the electric motor and gears

Questions

1 An electromagnet is a coil of wire through which a current can be passed.
   a) State three ways in which the strength of the electromagnet may be increased.
   b) An electromagnet can be switched on and off. Suggest one situation where this would be an advantage over a constant field permanent magnet.

2 The motor effect can be demonstrated using the apparatus shown in the diagram below. When a current is passed through the moveable brass rod, it rolls along the fixed brass rails.

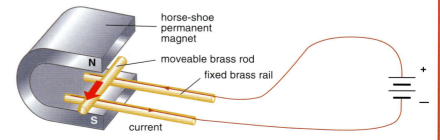

a) State the direction of the magnetic lines of force between the poles of the magnet.
b) In which direction will the rod roll?
c) The rod is placed back in its original position. What will happen to the rod if the poles of the magnet are reversed?
d) The rod is placed back in its original position. What will happen to the rod if the poles of the battery are reversed?

3 Below is a simplified diagram of a d.c. motor. The loop of wire is horizontal in a horizontal magnetic field.

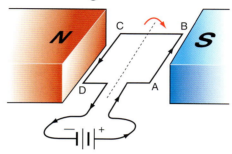

a) What does 'd.c.' mean?
b) In which direction is the force on side AB of the wire loop?
c) In which direction is the force on side CD of the wire loop?
d) Explain how these forces cause the loop to rotate.
e) What can you say about the force on side BC of the loop?

▶ Electromagnetic induction

In an electric motor, electricity is put into the coil producing motion. It was Michael Faraday who suggested that the process could be reversed – that electricity should be produced by moving a conductor through a magnetic field. This process is called **electromagnetic induction**.

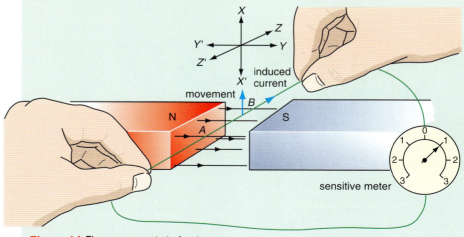

Figure 16 Electromagnetic induction

ELECTROMAGNETISM

Figure 16 shows an experiment to find out what affects the making of a current. It is found that there are two main factors:

* *Direction of movement* – to generate a current, the wire must cross lines of magnetic field. A current is produced if the wire is moved up and down along the direction XX'. But there is no current if the wire moves along ZZ' or YY'. Reversing the direction of movement reverses the current. So, if moving the wire up makes the pointer in the meter move to the right, then moving the wire down will make it go to the left.

* *Size of current* – the current generated can be increased in the following ways:
  * moving the wire more quickly
  * using stronger magnets
  * looping the wire so that several turns of wire pass through the poles.

It is also possible to induce a current by keeping the wire stationary and moving the magnetic field.

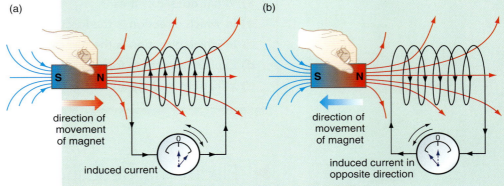

Figure 17 Inducing a current by moving the magnetic field

In Figure 17a, a current is generated by moving a magnet into a solenoid. When the current flows, a compass needle is attracted towards the right-hand end. So that end is behaving as a south pole and the left-hand end as a north pole. So, as the magnet moves towards the solenoid, there is a magnetic force that repels it, so you have to do some work to push the magnet into the solenoid. The work done in pushing the magnet generates the electrical energy.

In Figure 17b the magnet is being pulled out of the solenoid. The direction of the current is reversed and so there is now an attractive force acting on the magnet. The hand pulling the magnet is still doing work to produce electrical energy.

When a current is produced by electromagnetic induction, energy is always used to create the electrical energy. In the example described in Figure 17, the energy originally came from the muscles working the hand holding the magnet. So electromagnetic induction is just a way of converting mechanical energy to electrical energy. This is the principle behind electricity generation and transformers.

Figure 18 Airport security barriers are used to make sure that passengers aren't carrying guns or bombs. Metal objects cause changes in an electromagnetic field when they pass through the barrier. A circuit detects these changes and an alarm is set off

ELECTROMAGNETIC INDUCTION

Application of electromagnetic induction

A major application of electromagnetic induction is the **a.c. generator** (**alternator**).

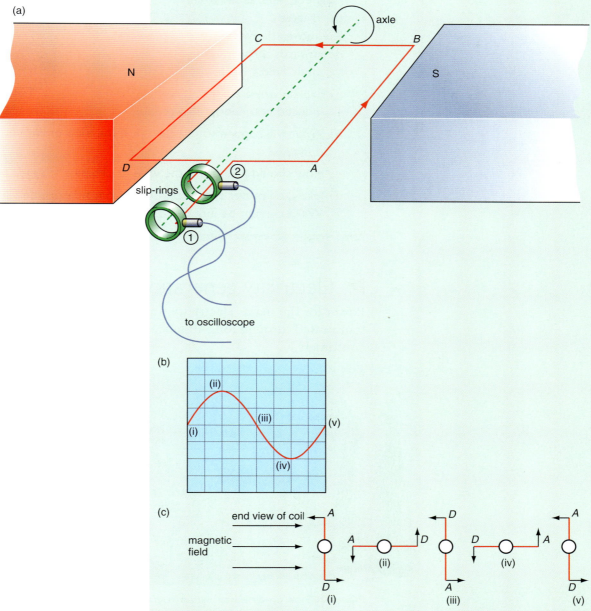

Figure 19 a An a.c. generator
b How the voltage waveform produced by the generator appears on an oscilloscope screen
c The position of the coil

Figure 19a shows the design of a very simple alternating current generator. When the axle is turned, a coil of wire moves through a magnetic field. This induces a voltage between the ends of the coil.

Figure 19b shows how the voltage waveform produced by the generator looks on an oscilloscope screen.

Figure 19b and 19c together match the various positions of the coil with the output voltage.

ELECTROMAGNETISM

Questions

4 Julie holds one loop of insulated copper wire in a magnetic field, as shown in the diagram. She moves the wire downwards through the magnetic field.

a) Explain why a current is induced in the loop of wire.

b) What will happen to the current if the loop of wire is moved upwards?

c) How should Julie move the wire to produce a bigger current?

d) Julie then moves the loop of wire from side to side. Will a current be induced? Explain your answer.

▶ Electricity generation and transmission

Power for the mains electricity supply is generated in power stations, transmitted through long-distance cables and then distributed to consumers.

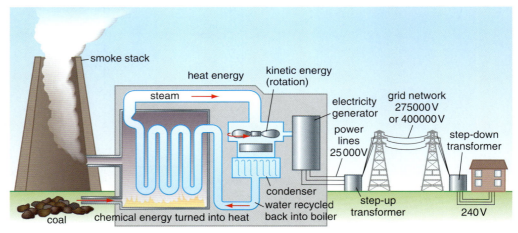

Figure 20 How power is transmitted from a power station, through the National Grid, to your home

Ballylumford Power Station contains four a.c. generators, each producing a current of 20 000 amps at a voltage of 33 000 volts. The current from each generator is fed to a huge step-up transformer which transfers power to overhead cables at a greatly increased voltage of 275 000 volts. The cables feed power to a nationwide supply network called the **grid**. Power from the grid is distributed by a series of **substations**. These contain step-down transformers which reduce the voltage in stages to the level needed by consumers. In the UK, for example, this is 230V for domestic consumers, although industry usually takes its power at a higher voltage.

⮕ DID YOU KNOW?

The world's largest coal-fired power station is the 4116 MW Kendal Power Station near Johannesburg. It can produce an amazing 4 116 000 000 joules of electrical energy every second.

ELECTRICITY GENERATION AND TRANSMISSION

Electricity transmission

Electrical power is distributed around the country from power stations through a grid of high-voltage power lines. The electricity in overhead power lines is transmitted to our homes and industry at 275 kV or 400 kV.

Figure 21 shows the National Grid for the UK. There are loops which ensure that when a local power station is switched off, electricity can still reach all the consumers in the area.

The National Grid in the UK is connected to the Northern Ireland grid and to the French grid. Southern Scotland sells excess electricity to Northern Ireland. France produces more electricity than it needs and sells large quantities to neighbouring countries.

Why use high voltages?

The high voltages used to transmit electrical power around a country are extremely dangerous. That is why the cables that carry the power are supported on tall pylons high above people, traffic and buildings. Sometimes the cables are buried underground, but this is much more expensive, and the cables must be safely insulated. High voltages are used because it means that the current flowing in the cables is relatively low, and this wastes less energy. This can be explained as follows.

When a current flows in a wire or cable, some of the energy it is carrying is lost because of the cable's resistance – the cables get hot. A small current wastes less energy than a high current. Consider the following two methods of transmitting electricity:

Figure 21 The National Grid for the UK

Method I

Let the resistance of the cable be 10 Ω, while carrying a current of 1000 A. Then

$R = 10\,\Omega$ power wasted in cables $= I^2R$

$I = 1000\,A$ $= 1000^2 \times 10$

                                              = 10 MW

Method II

Let the resistance of the cable be 10 Ω, while carrying a current of 100 A. Then

$R = 10\,\Omega$ power wasted in cables $= I^2R$

$I = 100\,A$ $= 100^2 \times 10$

                                              = 0.1 MW

Clearly, transmitting the smaller current reduces the heat lost in the cables dramatically.

Before electricity reaches homes the 400 000 V must be stepped down to 240 V because all domestic electrical appliances operate at 240 V – this is also for safety.

Transformers

Power stations typically generate electricity at 30 kV. This has to be converted to the grid voltage, usually 275 kV or 400 kV, using **transformers**.

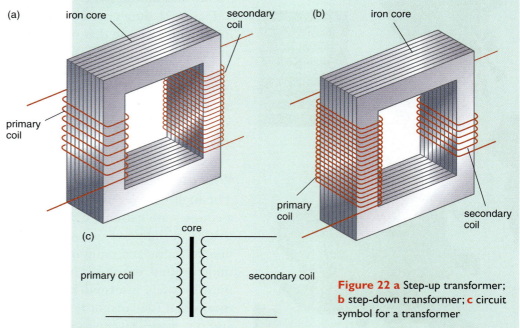

Figure 22 a Step-up transformer; **b** step-down transformer; **c** circuit symbol for a transformer

Figure 22a shows the construction of a transformer. It consists of two coils of wire wrapped round a laminated iron core. Figure 22b shows the construction of a step-down transformer – one that has fewer turns in the secondary coil than in the primary coil. Figure 22c shows the circuit symbol for a transformer.

All transformers have three parts:

* *Primary coil* – the incoming voltage V_p (voltage across primary coil) is connected across this coil.
* *Secondary coil* – this provides the output voltage V_s (voltage across the secondary coil) to the external circuit.
* *Laminated iron core* – this links the two coils magnetically.

There is no electrical connection between the two coils, which are constructed using insulated wire.

To step up the voltage by a factor of 10, there must be 10 times as many turns on the secondary coil as on the primary. The **turns ratio** tells us the factor by which the voltage will be changed.

* A step-up transformer increases the voltage – there are more turns on the secondary coil than on the primary.
* A step-down transformer decreases the voltage – there are fewer turns on the secondary coil than on the primary.

Note: according to the principle of conservation of energy, if the voltage is stepped up then the current must be stepped down and vice versa. The energy per second going into the transformer must equal the energy per second leaving the transformer.

Figure 23 This transformer delivers power to the National Grid

There is an important equation, known as the **transformer equation**, relating the two voltages V_p and V_s to the number of turns on each coil, N_p and N_s:

$$\frac{\text{voltage across primary coil}}{\text{number of turns in primary coil}} = \frac{\text{voltage across secondary coil}}{\text{number of turns in secondary coil}}$$

$$\frac{V_p}{N_p} = \frac{V_s}{N_s}$$

Example

A transformer is needed to step down the mains voltage at 240V to supply 20V. If the primary coil has 4800 turns, how many turns must the secondary coil have?

Answer

$V_p = 240\text{V}; V_s = 20\text{V}; N_p = 4800; N_s = ?$

$$\frac{V_p}{N_p} = \frac{V_s}{N_s}$$

$$\frac{240}{4800} = \frac{20}{N_s}$$

$$N_s = \frac{20 \times 4800}{240}$$

$$= \textbf{400 turns}$$

How transformers work

The alternating current in the primary coil converts the coil into an electromagnet, which produces an alternating magnetic field. The core transports this alternating field to the secondary coil. The secondary coil is now a conductor in a changing magnetic field. A current is therefore induced in the secondary coil. This type of electromagnetic induction is called mutual induction.

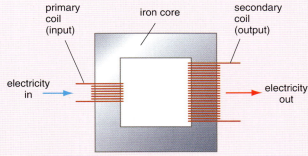

Figure 24 How a transformer works

It is important to realise that transformers convert alternating voltages from one form to another, but they do not work with d.c. If direct current is connected to a transformer, there is no output voltage. This is because the magnetic field produced by the primary coil does not change. With an unchanging field passing through the secondary coil, no voltage is induced.

ELECTROMAGNETISM

Questions

5. Why is electrical power transmitted in the grid at high voltage?
6. a) What are the three essential parts of a transformer?
   b) What is the purpose of the core of a transformer?
   c) Why must the core be made of soft iron?
7. Explain why a transformer will not work with direct current.
8. A step-down transformer changes 240V to 48V. There are 2000 turns on the primary coil. Find the number of turns on the secondary coil.
9. The diagram represents a simple transformer with 20 turns on the primary coil and 80 turns on the secondary coil. If 4V is supplied to the primary coil, what voltage would there be across the secondary?

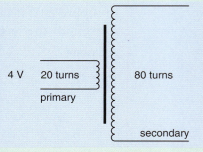

10. The voltage across the power lines supplying a house is 24 000V.

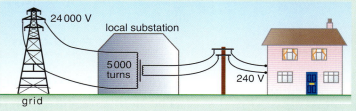

   a) What type of transformer must be used?
   b) Why is the supply not transmitted at 240V all the way?
   c) The 24 000V supply cannot be used unchanged in the house – why not?
   d) How many turns are there in the secondary coil of the local transformer?
11. An oil-fired power station produces electricity at 25 000V. This voltage is stepped up to 400 000V by a transformer.

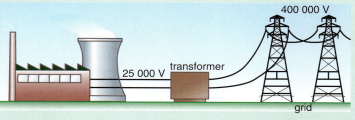

   a) What type of transformer is used between the power station and the National Grid?
   b) The number of turns in the primary coil of the transformer is 10 000. Calculate the number of turns in the secondary coil.
   c) Why is a voltage as high as 400 000V used in the transmission of electrical energy?

Search
- electromagnet
- electromagnetic relay
- circuit breakers
- electric motors
- a.c. generator
- electricity generation

Exam questions

1 Jo makes a model generator using the apparatus shown in the diagram below. Jo pulls down the bar magnet and then lets go. The magnet oscillates into and out of the coil.

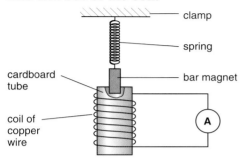

a) Explain why a current flows in the coil.
(2 marks)

b) Is the current in the coil alternating or direct? Give a reason for your answer.
(2 marks)

c) Copy the axes below and sketch the graph of current against time for the model generator above. *(2 marks)*

2 a) The diagram shows a simple transformer. The primary coil is connected to an a.c. supply.

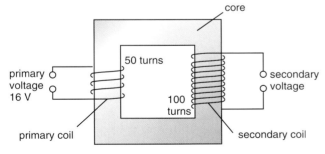

  i) What do the letters a.c. stand for? How is a.c. different from d.c.? *(3 marks)*
  ii) The primary and secondary coils are both wound on the same core. What is this core made of? *(1 mark)*
  iii) Using the information shown on the diagram, calculate the secondary voltage. Show clearly how you get your answer. *(4 marks)*

b) The diagram below shows the layout of a power pack that contains a transformer. The moveable switch can be turned so that it touches the contacts A to K.

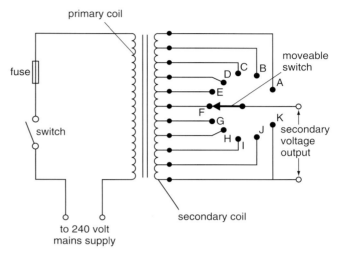

This allows the value of the secondary voltage to be varied. There are 50 turns of wire between consecutive pairs of terminals A to K – i.e. between A and B there are 50 turns, between B and C there are 50 turns, and so on.

  i) The maximum secondary voltage output of the power pack is 20V. In what voltage steps can the secondary voltage output be varied? Show clearly how you get your answer. *(3 marks)*
  ii) Calculate the total number of turns on the secondary coil. *(1 mark)*
  iii) Calculate how many turns of wire there must be on the 240V primary coil of this transformer. Show clearly how you get your answer. *(3 marks)*
  iv) Explain the function of the fuse. *(2 marks)*

c) The diagram below shows the main parts of a nuclear power station. Inside the nuclear reactor, nuclei undergo fission.

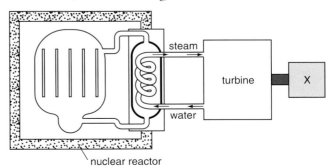

ELECTROMAGNETISM

i) What type of energy is produced by nuclei undergoing fission? *(2 marks)*

ii) Name the part marked X and state what it does. *(2 marks)*

d) The diagram below shows how electricity from the power station is distributed to homes.

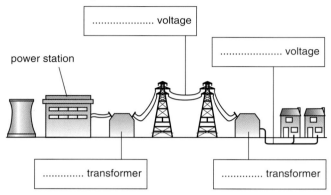

i) Copy the diagram and write the names of the types of transformer in the appropriate boxes. *(2 marks)*

ii) In the appropriate boxes on your diagram, label those parts of the distribution system where the voltage is high, and those parts where it is low. *(2 marks)*

iii) Why are high voltages used in the national distribution of electricity? *(2 marks)*

3 a) A coil carrying a current has two magnetic poles.

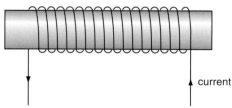

i) Copy the diagram and mark the magnetic poles produced. *(2 marks)*

ii) On your diagram, draw the magnetic field produced. *(4 marks)*

b) i) Draw a clearly-labelled diagram to show the construction of a step-up transformer. Indicate clearly where the input voltage is applied, and where output voltage is produced. *(7 marks)*

ii) Which of the following can be stepped up by a transformer?
   - a.c. voltages
   - d.c. voltages *(1 mark)*

iii) When 6V is applied to the primary coil of a transformer, 12V is produced at the secondary coil. If the primary coil has 200 turns, calculate the number of turns on the secondary coil. Show clearly how you get your answer. *(4 marks)*

c) Explain fully why the output of a power station is connected to a step-up transformer. *(4 marks)*

4 a) At a power station, the main transformer is supplied from a 25 kV generator.

i) How much energy is transferred from the generator for each coulomb of charge? *(1 mark)*

ii) The main transformer steps up the voltage to 275 kV before sending it out to the grid. Describe fully the purpose of stepping up the voltage. *(2 marks)*

iii) In what other part of the electricity transmission system must transformers be used? *(1 mark)*

iv) Why must these other transformers be used? *(1 mark)*

b) An electric shower has a power rating of 8000 W. It is switched on for 15 minutes.

i) How much energy, in kilowatt-hours, does the shower use? Show clearly how you obtain your answer. *(4 marks)*

ii) If one Unit of electricity costs 12p, calculate the cost of heating the water. Show clearly how you obtain your answer. *(1 mark)*

c) Two coils are placed side by side. A current meter is connected to one coil as shown in the diagram.

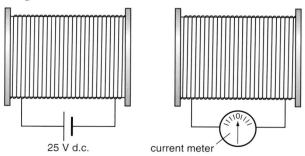

i) The first coil is connected to a 25V d.c. supply. Describe what happens to the meter reading:

1) when the first coil moves away from the second coil. *(1 mark)*
2) when the first coil moves back towards the second coil. *(2 marks)*

ii) The 25V d.c. supply is now replaced with a 25V a.c. 1 Hz supply connected to the first coil.

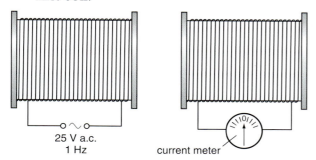

Describe fully what (if anything) happens to the meter reading if the first coil remains stationary. *(2 marks)*

8 The Earth and Universe

▶ The Solar System

We now know that the Earth is one of eight **planets** that travel around the Sun. Each planet travels in an elliptical path and, with the exception of Mercury and Venus, they all have at least one moon. Other objects also **orbit** the Sun. These are the **comets** and the **asteroids**. Table 1 below gives some data about the planets.

Planet	Planet diameter compared with Earth	Average distance of planet from Sun compared with Earth	Time to orbit the Sun compared with Earth	Number of moons
Mercury	0.4	0.4	0.2	0
Venus	0.9	0.7	0.6	0
Earth	1.0	1.0	1.0	1
Mars	0.5	1.5	1.9	2
Jupiter	11.2	5.2	12.0	14
Saturn	9.4	9.5	29.0	24
Uranus	4.1	19.1	84.0	15
Neptune	3.9	30.1	165.0	3

Table 1 Some data on the eight planets orbiting the Sun

> **DID YOU KNOW?**
>
> Every second, the total quantity of energy emitted from each square metre of the Sun's surface is approximately 63 000 000 joules – of this less than 400 joules reach each square metre of the Earth's surface.

Note that the status of Pluto was changed from a 'planet' to that of a 'dwarf planet' in 2005.

You are now expected to know that there are eight (not nine) planets in our Solar System.

The orbits of the inner planets are almost circular, with the Sun at the centre. The orbits of Jupiter, Saturn, Uranus and Neptune are much more elliptical (like a rugby ball). All the planets orbit the Sun in the same plane, as a result of the gravitational force between the Sun and the planets.

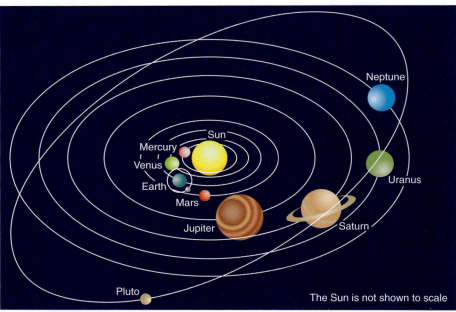

Figure 1 The Solar System

THE SOLAR SYSTEM

Heliocentric or geocentric?

The model of the **Solar System** just described is called a **heliocentric** model because it has the Sun at its centre. But the heliocentric model is only one of many that have been used to explain the motion of the planets across the sky. Most early models are **geocentric**, placing the Earth at the centre of the Universe.

About 500 BC, the Greek mathematician Pythagoras proposed a geocentric model. Pythagoras taught that the heavenly bodies orbited the Earth on crystal spheres – the inner spheres carried the Moon and the planets; the outer sphere, called the celestial sphere, carried the stars. He believed that the closer a sphere was to the Earth, the slower it rotated. This model allowed Pythagoras to explain the motion of the Sun, the Moon and the planets as seen from Earth. Unfortunately the model was unable to explain why some planets, like Jupiter, appear to make strange loops as they travel across the sky.

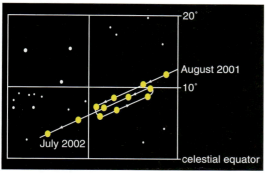

Figure 2 This simulation shows Jupiter's retrograde loop during 2001 and 2002. The position of Jupiter is marked at 1-month intervals

Around AD 120, the Egyptian astronomer Ptolemy put forward an idea to explain why some planets show their strange motion across the sky. Like Pythagoras, Ptolemy believed that the Earth was at the centre of the Universe. Ptolemy also believed that the planets orbited the Earth in 'epicycles' – Figure 3 applies Ptolemy's idea to Jupiter.

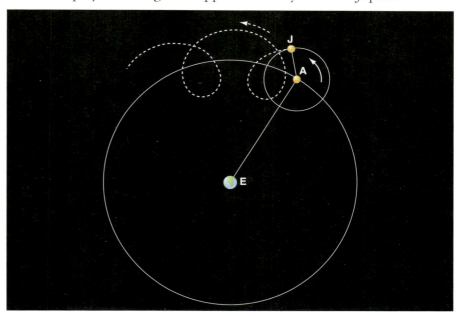

Figure 3 Ptolemy explained the loops of planets with this construction of 'epicycles'

Arm EA rotates around the Earth every 12 years, but at the same time arm AJ rotates around A once a year. The position of Jupiter (J) is the result of the combined movement of EA and AJ.

What is wrong with Ptolemy's model? The main problem is that Ptolemy's system was not based on experimental evidence and observation, and the planetary motion it describes appears highly unlikely. In addition, there were so many other things that the model could not explain. Why did the Moon show phases? Why was it that sometimes Venus was brighter than Mars, and sometimes Mars was brighter than Venus?

All this changed when Nicholas Copernicus put forward a revolutionary idea in the early part of the sixteenth century. Copernicus' model placed the Sun at the centre of our Solar System, with the planets in orbit around it. Copernicus explained the different shapes (phases) of the Moon by saying that it was in orbit around the Earth. After careful observation of the planets, Copernicus was able to prove convincingly that the order of the planets from the Sun was as they are listed today.

Copernicus was also able to:

* explain that the apparent 'looping' of planets was due to the combined motion of the Earth and the planet itself
* explain that at some times Venus is closer to Earth than Mars so it appears brighter, but at other times Venus is further away than Mars and appears less bright
* predict that Venus and Mercury should show phases, just as our Moon does.

Then, in 1610, an Italian astronomer, Galileo Galilei, used a new invention called the telescope to observe the planets. Just as Copernicus had predicted, Galileo observed the phases of Venus. When he turned his telescope to Jupiter, he saw what he first took to be new stars. But if they were stars, their motion was very strange indeed – they appeared to change position over just a few hours. It did not take long for Galileo to realise that what he was looking at were some of Jupiter's many moons.

Galileo firmly believed in the heliocentric model put forward by Copernicus. But many opposed him and none was more powerful than the Pope. In the seventeenth century, the Church taught that the Earth was the centre of God's creation and strongly disapproved of those who believed otherwise. Galileo was eventually imprisoned in his own home and was forced to keep his new ideas to himself. Only after many years did the Church change its position and admit that our Solar System is heliocentric and is arranged as Galileo and Copernicus believed. Then, as today, the acceptance or rejection of scientific theories by some people depends on the prevailing social climate.

Satellites

'Satellite' is the name given to a body that orbits another body. The eight planets in the Solar System along with their moons, the comets and the asteroids are all natural satellites of the Sun. The moons are natural satellites of the planets that they orbit. Artificial satellites are those placed in orbit around the Earth by man. Artificial satellites have four main purposes:

* communications
* Earth observation
* astronomy
* weather monitoring.

THE DOPPLER EFFECT

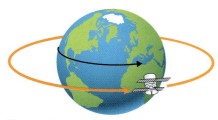

Figure 4 A geosynchronous satellite

Geostationary satellites

These can also be called geosynchronous satellites. They are placed about 36 000 km above the Equator and take exactly 24 hours to orbit the Earth. The Earth also takes 24 hours to spin on its axis. So, to an observer on the Earth these satellites appear to be standing still – hence the name 'geostationary'. 'Geosynchronous' means having the same orbit time as the Earth.

This makes them ideal for telephone and TV communications and for global positioning systems (for use in SatNavs) because they are always in the same place relative to the Earth. Communications satellites can transfer radio and microwave signals from one side of the Earth to another in a fraction of a second. Remember that in space all electromagnetic waves travel at 300 million metres per second.

Figure 5 A low polar orbit satellite

Low polar orbit satellites

In a low polar orbit, the satellite sweeps over both poles while the Earth rotates beneath it. The time taken for each full orbit of the satellite is just a few hours. Each time the satellite comes round it can scan a different part of the Earth. This means that the whole surface of the planet can be monitored each day.

Satellites in low polar orbits are ideal for taking photographs for weather forecasting, for spying on military installations or for monitoring movements in the ice sheets at the North and South Poles to advance our knowledge of global warming.

Satellites in astronomy

A big advantage of having telescopes on satellites is that they can take photographs without the blurring caused by the Earth's atmosphere. This allows much greater detail to be seen of the planets in the Solar System and of distant stars and galaxies. It also allows us to take photographs in the X-ray, ultraviolet, infrared and radio wave parts of the spectrum.

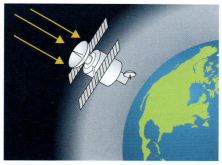

Figure 6

The Doppler effect

Think about what we hear when a police car passes with its siren sounding. As the car approaches, the sound appears to have a higher pitch (or lower wavelength) than we would expect. But as soon as the car passes, its pitch falls. This is called the **Doppler effect**.

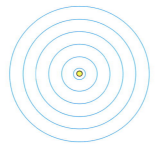
source of sound at rest

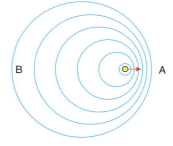
source of sound moving to the right

Figure 7 The Doppler effect

The sound source on the right is moving to the right. Observer A hears sound of high pitch (low wavelength) because the waves are being bunched up together. Observer B, to the left of the source, hears a sound of low pitch (high wavelength) because the waves are being spread out.

A similar effect occurs with light. If the light that we observe from a moving source has a shorter wavelength than expected, it is because the source is moving towards us – we say the light is 'blue shifted'. But if the light we observe has a longer wavelength than expected, it is because the source is moving away from us – and we say the light is 'red shifted'.

▶ Composition of light

Visible light consists of much more than seven different colours. Physicists prefer to think that there is a continuum from red to violet – so there is an infinite number of colours in the visible spectrum.

Each colour has a wavelength associated with it. Colours in the red end of the spectrum have wavelengths around 700 nm; colours in the violet region have a wavelength around 450 nm. (1 nm = 1×10^{-9} m = 1 billionth of a metre.) So, the visible spectrum consists of all those electromagnetic waves with a wavelength from about 450 nm to about 700 nm.

Figure 8 Absorption spectrum for hydrogen

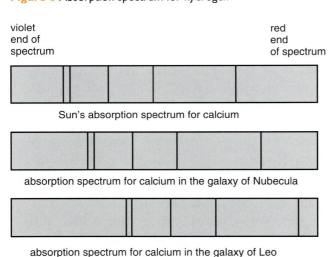

Figure 9 Absorption spectra from different galaxies

Our Sun contains hydrogen. We know this because there are black lines in the spectrum of the light from the Sun, where hydrogen atoms have absorbed light. This pattern of black lines is called the **absorption spectrum** for hydrogen.

By closely examining the spectrum of the light coming from the Sun, physicists have identified over 50 different elements in it, but hydrogen and helium are by far the most abundant.

What happens when we look at the light from the stars in distant galaxies? Do we get the same pattern as we do from the Sun? The answer is that the pattern is the same, but it is shifted towards the red end of the spectrum (Figure 9). This is an example of the Doppler effect and is called **red-shift**. The pattern of the absorption spectrum stays the same, but it appears to have moved closer to the red end of the spectrum.

How do we interpret these strange absorption spectrum data? If there is a red-shift in the light from another galaxy, this tells us that the source is moving away from us. The fact that we always get red-shift from the distant galaxies tells us that the galaxies are all moving away from us. This is what we mean when we say the Universe is expanding.

The greater red-shift in the light from the Leo galaxy in Figure 9 suggests that Leo is moving away from our galaxy (the Milky Way) at a greater speed than Nubecula.

▶ Background radiation

Between the galaxies there is very little matter – on average perhaps only a single atom in every cubic centimetre. But if radio telescopes are directed at these areas of space, the atoms appear to give off microwave radiation. The wavelength of this radiation appears to be the same no matter where it occurs. What is astonishing is that such a wavelength corresponds to a temperature of about −270 °C or 3 Kelvin. It is therefore called '3 K continuous background radiation'. But why is it there? To answer that question we must ask how the Universe came into being.

▶ Big Bang theory

Almost all physicists now accept the **Big Bang theory** as the most likely explanation for the origin of the Universe. Red-shift tells us that all the galaxies are currently travelling away from us at very great speed. It is then argued that at some time in the distant past they must have been much closer together. Going back far enough in time, they must have been in the same place. This led to the idea that the Universe originated with an enormous cosmic explosion – the Big Bang.

According to most physicists, the Big Bang occurred between 12 000 and 15 000 million years ago. It certainly was not an explosion of the conventional type, because it was only then that matter, energy and time came into existence. What is confidently accepted is that the Big Bang came from a tiny point that physicists call a **singularity**.

Not long after the Big Bang, the Universe was made up of high-energy radiation and elementary particles like quarks, the particles that make up protons and neutrons. This was a period of rapid expansion or 'inflation'. Rapid expansion is always associated with cooling, so as the Universe got bigger it cooled down. This allowed the quarks to come together to form protons and neutrons. Further expansion and cooling allowed isotopes of hydrogen to form. Eventually the temperature dropped enough for electrons to combine with neutrons and protons to form atoms of hydrogen.

In the 1960s two American physicists, Arno Penzias and Bob Wilson, discovered microwaves coming from all parts of the sky. Today most physicists believe that this continuous, background microwave radiation is the remnant or 'echo' of the Big Bang. The existence of this cosmic microwave background radiation (CMBR) is further evidence of the Big Bang. Indeed, the Big Bang is currently the only model that explains CMBR.

Steady State theory

Few scientists today accept the Steady State theory – this is based on the idea that the Universe looks much the same everywhere, and always has done. It suggests that the Universe had no beginning and will have no end. In order to explain the expansion of the Universe, this theory suggests that matter is being created continually. Physicists are uncomfortable with this idea because it suggests that our thoughts about energy conservation might not be correct. In addition, the theory fails to explain why the Universe is expanding or why there is cosmic microwave background radiation.

▶ How are stars and planets formed?

Stars form when clouds of hydrogen, known as a **stellar nebula**, come together because of gravity. As these clouds become more and more dense, they start to spiral inwards and the temperature rises enormously. Gravity eventually compresses the hydrogen so much that the temperature reaches about 15 million °C. At this temperature, nuclear fusion reactions start and a star is born. The energy from the nuclear fusion is emitted as light and other radiation.

At the same time, other clouds of gas and dust come together, but may not have enough material for the temperature to reach 15 million °C. Such gas and dust clouds are called **planetary nebulae** and eventually they become planets as a result of gravitational attraction. This clumping together of gas and dust is called **accretion**. The presence of a massive star may cause them to become trapped in its orbit. Since the gas and dust clouds originally spiralled in the same direction, so the planets would orbit the Sun in the same way.

Why are the inner planets rocky while the outer planets are gaseous?

It seems that as soon as the Sun began to shine, its radiation 'blew' much of the gas away to the outer reaches of the Solar System. Here the gas collected by gravitation to form the outer planets. However, the dust particles, being of greater mass, were not 'blown' so far and, over millions of years, gravitational accretion caused the dust to form the inner, rocky planets.

Interestingly, all the planets orbit the Sun in the same plane. Pluto, the 'dwarf planet', has an orbit that intersects with the plane of the orbits of the other planets. This has led astronomers to believe that Pluto did not come into existence at the same time as the rest of the planets. One view is that Pluto used to be a 'wandering body', which drifted into the Solar System and became trapped in the gravitational field of the Sun.

Asteroids are small, rocky objects in the Solar System and almost all of them are found between the orbits of Mars and Jupiter. Some astronomers believe that they were formed as a result of a collision between larger objects – some asteroids may be extinct comets. More than 5000 have been studied in detail, although many astronomers believe there may be over 10 000 asteroids in total. A common theory is that the asteroids are the rocky structures that come together over millions of years to form planets, but that this did not happen in the case of the asteroids in the Solar System because of the enormous gravitational pull of Jupiter.

Comets are sometimes called dirty snowballs. At their centre is rock, ice, silicates and some organic compounds – surrounding this is a 'coma' consisting of gases and dust. Most comets orbit the Sun in very elliptical paths. As a comet approaches the Sun, solar radiation vaporises some of the frozen gas at the centre causing the coma greatly to increase in size. Dust and gas stream away from the comet as a long tail, often millions of kilometres long. The radiation from the Sun causes this tail to point away from the Sun at the comet's closest approach. Most astronomers believe that comets in our Solar System originate in the Oort cloud, a region of space between 2000 and 3000 times further from the Sun than Pluto.

▶ Nuclear fusion

Stars like the Sun are made up almost entirely of **hydrogen nuclei**. Being positively charged, these nuclei normally repel each other. However, the temperature near the centre of the Sun is so high that nuclei collide with each other at unbelievably high speeds. When they collide at such speeds they can form new, heavier nuclei such as helium-3 and helium-4. This process is called **nuclear fusion** and results in the production of vast quantities of heat and light energy.

The stability of the Sun

Our Sun was formed about 4.5 billion years ago and is expected to be around for another 5.5 billion years. Even though it is converting mass into energy at a rate of about 4 million tonnes per second, its apparent size in the sky has remained the same for as long as mankind has been on Earth. You might have expected the yellow disc that we see in the sky to be getting smaller and smaller as time passes, but this is not the case.

The reason is because the force of gravity, which pulls inwards towards the centre, exactly balances the outward force (called **radiation 'pressure'**) due to the thermonuclear explosions occurring there.

> **DID YOU KNOW?**
>
> While the centre of the Sun is at a temperature of around 15 000 000 °C, its surface is only around 6000 °C and some parts of its corona, about 75 000 km above the surface, are around 2 000 000 °C. Exactly why this is so remains a mystery.

> **DID YOU KNOW?**
>
> At its centre, the Sun is so dense that a teaspoonful of solar matter has the same mass as about 15 aircraft carriers, each of 100 000 tonnes.

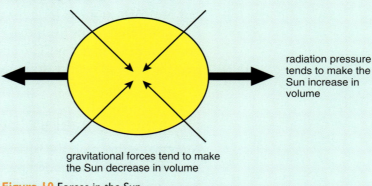

Figure 10 Forces in the Sun

THE EARTH AND UNIVERSE

▶ The future of the Universe

Physicists speculate that there may be three ways in which the Universe may come to an end.

* **Big freeze** – if there is not enough mass for the force of gravity to stop the Universe expanding, then the expansion will continue forever. As the galaxies get further and further apart, their gravitational potential energy increases, but they get colder and colder.

* **Big crunch** – if there is enough mass in the Universe, then the force of gravity will be enough to stop the Universe expanding and eventually to cause it to collapse on itself. The galaxies will move towards each other with increasing speed, eventually crashing into each other with unimaginable force.

* **Big bounce** – some physicists have suggested that gravity may eventually be big enough to bring matter so close together that conditions will be similar to those not long after the Big Bang. If further contraction occurs, the Universe may collapse to another singularity and another Big Bang can occur. According to this idea, the Universe is destined to repeatedly crunch, bang, crunch and so on.

What is undeniable is that the ultimate end of the Universe depends on the amount of mass and energy it contains. Astrophysicists today talk of dark matter and dark energy – matter and energy that we suspect may be there, but which we cannot observe directly.

Evidence for planets outside our Solar System

There is now undeniable evidence that there are planets orbiting stars outside our Solar System – by the end of 2010, about 400 such planets had been discovered. Of course, it is not known if these planets can support life as we know it. However, it is increasingly thought that there are likely to be very many other planets, some of which have the potential to support life.

How are planets outside our Solar System detected? This is often done by observing the light coming from stars that are similar to our Sun. Astronomers look for a 'transition' – a tiny reduction in the light reaching us from that star when an orbiting planet passes between the star and us. The effect is very small, but to the trained astrophysicist the effect is unmistakeable.

▶ Space travel in the Solar System

Man first set foot on the surface of the Moon in 1969, and although there have been unmanned probes to all of the other planets in the Solar System, humans have never ventured further than the Moon.

SPACE TRAVEL IN THE SOLAR SYSTEM

There is currently an American plan to put a human on the surface of Mars by 2020, although there are scientific, engineering and financial issues which make it unlikely that this target date will be achieved.

How far is it to the nearest star?

A **light year** is the distance travelled by light in a year. Light travels at 300 000 000 metres per second. So 1 light year is 300 000 000 × 365 × 24 × 60 × 60 metres away – this is a staggering distance.

The nearest star to Earth (other than our Sun) is called Proxima Centauri. It is approximately 4.2 light years away. Our fastest spacecraft can travel at a maximum speed of 70 000 m/s. At this speed it would take a staggering 18 000 years to reach Proxima Centauri, or any planet in orbit about it.

The vast distances to the stars mean that it is certain that with our present technology it is not currently feasible to visit any planet outside our Solar System. There are insurmountable difficulties:

* *flight time* – the distance is so great that the flight would last for many generations
* *engineering* – our spacecraft are just too slow
* *logistics* – it is not clear how the spacecraft could carry enough fuel, oxygen and water
* *ethical* – the chance of failure would be high, with no possibility of return to Earth.

If there is life on other planets, we are most likely to detect it using large arrays of radio telescopes. How do scientists carry out the search for extra-terrestrial intelligence (SETI)? Broadly speaking, they look for non-random radio signals coming from distant star systems – it is rather like trying to pick up EastEnders from space!

Questions

1 Write the following objects in order of increasing size:
   star   planet   asteroid   galaxy   Universe
2 a) What is 'red-shift'?
  b) What does red-shift tell us about neighbouring galaxies?
3 List the planets in order as you travel away from the Sun.
4 Why do people believe that the planets orbit the Sun?
5 What does the Big Bang theory have to say about the origin of the Universe?
6 Why is the Steady State theory unpopular at the moment?
7 What is nuclear fusion and where does it occur in the Universe?
8 How did the planets come into existence?
9 According to current estimates, how old is the Universe?

The structure of the Earth

Crust, mantle, outer and inner core

The Earth has an 'onion' structure consisting of four layers – a solid outer **crust** floats on a thick, viscous **mantle**, while a liquid **outer core** surrounds a dense, solid, **inner core**. The description 'viscous' means that the mantle is a liquid, in the same way that cold treacle is – it doesn't flow easily.

The crust is very thin – about 20 km or so on average – and is mainly basalt rock. Beneath the oceans, the crust is between 5 and 11 km thick, while beneath the continents it ranges from about 20 to just over 60 km in depth.

The mantle lies below the crust and is around 2900 km thick. It consists mainly of silica and minerals of iron, magnesium and other metals. The Earth's **lithosphere** is the lower part of the crust and the upper, solid part of the upper mantle.

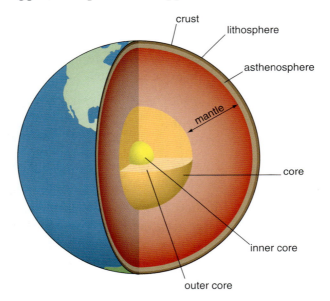

Figure 11 The Earth's structure

The core extends to just over half the Earth's radius. It is made from iron and nickel – and is where the Earth's magnetic field originates.

The overall density of the Earth is about 5.5 g/cm^3, which is much lower than the density of common rocks. This means that the inside must be made of something denser than rock. Iron and nickel are very dense metals – their presence in the core explains the high average density of the Earth. Also, they are both magnetic materials and account for the fact that Earth has a magnetic field round it.

By following the paths of earthquake waves as they travel through the Earth, we can tell that there is a change from solid to liquid about halfway through the Earth. This is why we believe that the outer core is liquid. Earthquake waves also indicate that the Earth has a solid inner core.

It is now generally believed that it is radioactive decay that creates all the heat inside the Earth. This heat causes the convection currents, which cause the plates of the crust to move.

THE STRUCTURE OF THE EARTH

The Earth's surface is made of large plates of rock

The Earth's lithosphere is the crust and the upper part of the mantle. It is cracked into pieces called **plates**. These plates are like big rafts that float across the liquid mantle. Figure 12 shows the edges of these plates. As they move, the continents move too. The plates are moving very slowly, at a speed of about 1 or 2 cm per year.

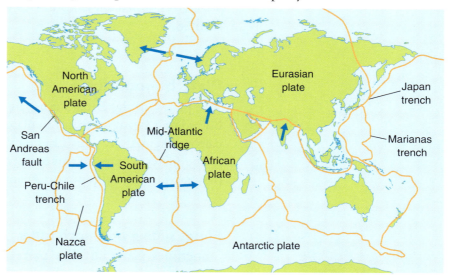

Figure 12 The Earth's tectonic plates

An early theory was that all the features of the Earth's surface, such as mountains and valleys, were due to shrinkage of the crust as it cooled. However, in 1915 Alfred Wegener proposed a theory of 'continental drift'. This suggested that the continents had once been joined and that they were slowly drifting apart. At first the theory was rejected, mainly because Wegener could not provide convincing evidence. Only in the 1960s with fossil evidence and the magnetic pattern in the mid-Atlantic ridge was the theory more widely accepted. Today it is more common to talk about the movement of 'plates' on the Earth's surface rather than 'continental drift' and the new theory is usually called **plate tectonics**. The word 'tectonic' simply means 'within the crust of the Earth'.

What is the evidence in favour of plate tectonics and continental drift? There's a very obvious **jigsaw fit** between Africa and South America. The other continents can also be fitted together. It's now widely believed that they once all formed a single land mass called **Pangea,** about 250 million years ago.

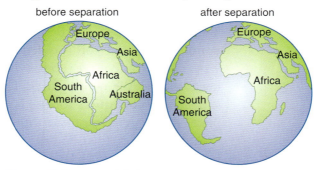

Figure 13 Continental drift

THE EARTH AND UNIVERSE

By 180 million years ago, this supercontinent had broken up into Gondwanaland (South America, Africa, Australia and Antarctica) and Laurasia (North America and Eurasia). By 65 million years ago, the present pattern of our continents was established.

Other evidence comes from rock strata. When rock strata of similar ages are studied in various countries, they show remarkable similarity – suggesting that these countries were joined together when the rocks formed.

Plate boundaries

The plates on the Earth's crust are called tectonic plates. At the boundaries between tectonic plates there is usually volcanic and/or earthquake activity. This can be explained in terms of the movement of the plates. There are three different ways that plates interact – sliding past each other, colliding or separating.

Plates sliding past each other

Sometimes, plates just slide past each other. The best known example of this is the San Andreas Fault in California (Figure 14).

A narrow strip of the coastline (along the edge of the Nazca plate) is sliding north while the North American plate is sliding south. Big plates of rock don't glide past each other smoothly – they catch on each other and as the forces build up they can suddenly lurch and cause an **earthquake**. This sudden lurching lasts only a few seconds – but it can bring buildings down.

The city of San Francisco sits astride this fault line. The city was destroyed by an earthquake in 1906 and hit by another one in 1989. San Francisco could have another any time. In earthquake zones they try to build earthquake-proof buildings that are designed to withstand a bit of shaking.

Earthquakes usually cause much greater devastation in poorer countries where there may be overcrowded cities, poorly constructed buildings and inadequate rescue services.

Figure 14

Oceanic and continental plates colliding

What happens when an oceanic and a continental plate collide? The oceanic plate is less dense and is always forced underneath the continental plate – this is called a **subduction zone** (Figure 15).

As the oceanic crust is pushed down, it melts and pressure builds up because of all the melting rock. This molten rock finds its way to the surface and **volcanoes** form. There can also be earthquakes as the two plates slowly grind past each other.

A deep trench forms on the ocean floor where the oceanic plate is being forced down. The continental crust crumples and folds, forming mountains along the coast.

THE STRUCTURE OF THE EARTH

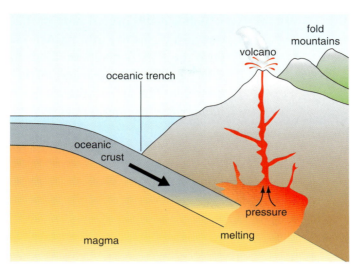

Figure 15

The classic example of all this is found along the west coast of South America where the Andes mountains are. That region has all these features – volcanoes, earthquakes, oceanic trench and mountains.

Tectonic plates moving apart

Earthquakes and volcanoes under the sea can cause devastating tsunami, such as the one which struck Banda Ache in 2000. These waves can cause great destruction when they reach land.

When tectonic plates move apart, magma (molten rock) rises from the mantle to fill the gap and produces new crust made of basalt rock. Sometimes it comes out with great force producing undersea volcanoes. As the magma rises up through the gap, it forms **ridges** and underwater mountains (Figure 16). These form a symmetrical pattern either side of the ridge – providing strong evidence for the theory of continental drift.

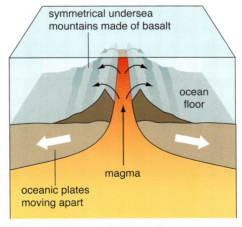

Figure 16 Ocean ridge formation

The Mid-Atlantic ridge runs the whole length of the Atlantic Ocean (Figure 17) and actually cuts through the middle of Iceland, which is why they have hot underground water.

The most compelling evidence in favour of continental drift comes from the magnetic orientation of the rocks in under-ocean ridges,

Figure 17 The Mid-Atlantic ridge

which was discovered only in the 1960s. As the liquid magma erupts out of the gap, the iron particles in the rocks tend to align themselves with the Earth's magnetic field, and as it cools they set in that position. Every half million years or so, the Earth's magnetic field tends to swap direction. This means the rocks on either side of the ridge have bands of alternate magnetic polarity.

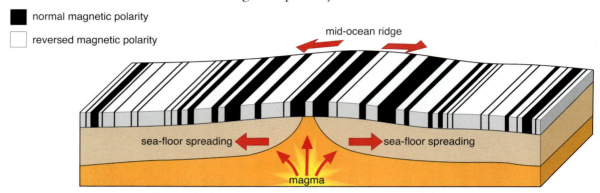

Figure 18 Alternating magnetic orientations

This pattern is found to be symmetrical either side of the ridge. These magnetic stripes (and hence the growth of the crust) spread out at a rate of about 2 cm per year – much the same speed as your fingernails grow.

Questions

10 What is the evidence in favour of plate tectonics and continental drift?
11 Why are there so many earthquakes at locations where tectonic plates meet?
12 What is the lithosphere?
13 Assume that two continents are moving apart at a rate of 1.2 cm per year. Calculate how far, in km, they move apart in 50 000 centuries (five million years).

Exam questions

1 Photographs from the Hubble telescope show distant objects in the Universe. Some of them are spinning gas clouds.

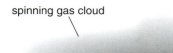
spinning gas cloud

a) i) Give another name for a gas cloud. *(1 mark)*

ii) What does the spinning gas cloud consist of (apart from gas particles)? *(1 mark)*

iii) What happens gradually to the material in the spinning gas cloud as time passes? *(1 mark)*

iv) What will eventually be formed in the spinning gas cloud after millions of years? *(1 mark)*

b) i) Name the nuclear process that powers a star. *(1 mark)*

ii) Name one type of energy produced by this nuclear process. *(1 mark)*

2 The Solar System contains eight planets. Copy and complete the table below. *(4 marks)*

Planet	Distance from Sun in millions of kilometres
Earth	150
	778
Mercury	58
	108
Uranus	2870
Neptune	4497
	142
Saturn	228

3 The Solar System forms part of a galaxy. The galaxy is part of a larger system.

a) What is the name of the larger system? *(1 mark)*

b) The following diagram shows the eight planets that orbit the Sun.

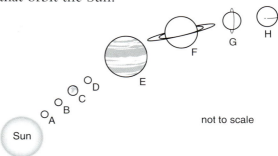
not to scale

i) Name the planet that is furthest from the Sun. *(1 mark)*

Use the letters A to G to answer the following two questions.

ii) Which planet is the Earth? *(1 mark)*

iii) Between which planets would you encounter most asteroids? *(1 mark)*

iv) Name the four giant planets – E, F, G and H. *(2 marks)*

c) The Sun emits radiation. What nuclear process takes place in the Sun to enable it to emit radiation? *(1 mark)*

d) Man has visited the Moon on several occasions. Explain fully why no one has visited Mars, which is much further away. *(2 marks)*

e) There are two scientific theories describing the formation of the Universe. One is the Big Bang theory – name the other theory. *(1 mark)*

f) How does the Big Bang theory describe:
  i) the beginning of the Universe *(1 mark)*
  ii) the Universe at present? *(1 mark)*

4 The diagram below shows the model of the Solar System used over 2000 years ago by the Ancient Greeks. Their model had five planets, the Moon and the Sun all orbiting the Earth.

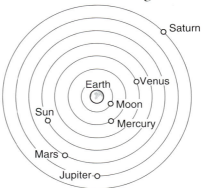

THE EARTH AND UNIVERSE

a) State two differences between our present model of the Solar System and that used by the Ancient Greeks. *(2 marks)*

b) The nebular, or gas cloud, model is often used to describe how our Solar System was formed. Describe the main stages that took place during the formation of the Solar System according to this model. *(2 marks)*

c) The diagram below shows the path of a comet as it approaches the Sun.

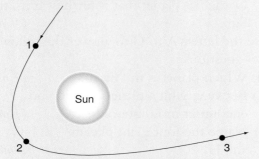

i) Copy the diagram, and draw an arrow to show the direction of the force acting on the comet at positions 1, 2 and 3. *(3 marks)*

ii) What causes this force? *(1 mark)*

iii) What can you say about the size of this force at position 1 compared to position 2? Explain your answer. *(2 marks)*

iv) As it moves along the path shown, the comet has gravitational potential energy. What other type of energy does it possess? *(1 mark)*

v) What happens to the gravitational potential energy of the comet as it moves from position 1 to position 2? Does the potential energy increase, stay the same or decrease? *(1 mark)*

vi) At position 2, the comet is moving faster than at position 1. Explain in terms of energy why this is so. *(2 marks)*

5 The light from the stars in galaxies other than our own is observed to be red-shifted.

a) What is meant by red-shift? *(1 mark)*

b) What does red-shift tell us about the motion of these galaxies? *(2 marks)*

6 a) Our Sun contains helium. We know this because there are black lines in the spectrum of the light from the Sun, where helium atoms have absorbed light. These lines form the absorption spectrum shown below for helium.

When we look at the spectrum of light from stars in a distant galaxy, the absorption spectrum of helium is there, but the pattern of lines has moved towards one end of the spectrum, as shown in the next diagram.

i) What name is given to the observation described above? *(1 mark)*

ii) The above observation provides evidence that distant galaxies are moving relative to us. In what direction are these galaxies moving? *(1 mark)*

One theory suggests that about 13.6 billion years ago, all the matter in the Universe was concentrated into a single tiny point.

b) What name is given to this theory? *(1 mark)*

c) Describe the nebular model for the formation of our Solar System. *(4 marks)*

d) Describe the nuclear process that happens in the interior of our Sun. *(3 marks)*

Controlled Assessment Task

▶ The task

Whether you are taking GCSE Physics or DAS (Physics), the Controlled Assessment Task (CAT) is exactly the same. It has three parts:

* Part A is concerned with Planning and Risk Assessment
* Part B is about Data Collection
* Part C is concerned with Processing, Analysis and Evaluation.

All this work must be done in school – you will not be permitted to take the material home. The total mark for the CAT is 45.

Part A: Planning and risk assessment

You will be given a short scenario and be asked to plan an investigation that relates in some way to your course. The plan and risk assessment together are worth 18 marks.

You need to consider very carefully how you propose to carry out the investigation. Your written work should include:

* your *background knowledge* of the topic
* a *hypothesis* – this is your idea as to what you think your investigation will show
* a *detailed explanation* as to the reason for your hypothesis
* a suitable *apparatus list* and how it will be assembled
* an identification of the *key factors* you will vary, measure and control – these are sometimes called the independent, dependent and controlled variables
* a blank *table* with appropriately labelled headings for your experimental results
* a detailed *method* describing what you plan to do
* a *statement* about what you propose to do with your results to prove your hypothesis is true or false.

In this section you should be able to plan how you are going to carry out the task and state a **hypothesis** (what you think your results will show). Remember, your hypothesis is a prediction – what you predict may not necessarily happen. This is not a problem so long as your prediction is a reasonable one based on the background information you bring to your planning.

To gain full marks in this section you need to be able to develop a hypothesis but also explain why you have produced your hypothesis. You should use scientific knowledge and terminology relevant to the topic under consideration.

The plan you devise will need to be **valid** — it will test what you are asked to do and will allow you to accept or reject your hypothesis. It also needs to produce **reliable** results — reliability is affected by both the **range** of results you plan to collect and also the **number** of results (including repeats where appropriate).

Part of the plan is to do some risk assessment. This means you will have to consider the safety aspects of your plan, identify the dangers and state what you propose to do to minimise the risk to yourself and your fellow students.

The Plan and Risk Assessment are then collected by your teacher and marked. What happens next depends on how well you do in Part A.

Part B: Data collection

If your plan is OK, or needs only very small changes, your teacher will tell you so and you will go on to carry out your investigation by doing one or more experiments and recording your results. However, sometimes your teacher will have to amend your plan. This might be because your proposed method won't work, or perhaps it is too dangerous, or maybe there is limited apparatus of the type you want to use. If this is so, your teacher will give you a new plan and ask you to use it, rather than your original plan. Before you start doing any experimental work you should be clear in your mind exactly what you intend to do, how you will set up the apparatus, the measurements you propose to make, how you propose to record your results and what you propose to do with them to confirm the hypothesis. Your results should be recorded in the blank table you drew in Part A.

It may surprise you to learn that there are **no marks for the data collection** part of your investigation. However, you do need to collect data because it is almost certain that you will be asked to do something in Part C with the numbers obtained.

Part C: Processing, analysis and evaluation

This is **very like an ordinary examination** and it must be done by you *alone*, without help from fellow pupils. You may be asked to plot a suitable graph to show the data you collected in Part B and to draw conclusions based on it. You may also be asked questions about how you kept the controlled factors constant and other details relating to your experiment. You will generally be given some **external data** on which you must do some calculations or describe trends.

Finally, you will be asked to do a piece of extended writing on some topic related to your investigation. In this, you will be assessed on the quality of the science in your response and on your written communication skills — including the use of science terms.

Part C is worth 27 marks (around 60% of the entire CAT), so it is important that you get as much practice as you can on this type of activity.

Index

absorption spectrum 164
acceleration 3–4, 7
   mass and 14–16, 20
a.c. generators 151
air bags 20
air resistance 9
alpha radiation 59, 61, 68
alternating current 133
ammeters 114
amplitude 75, 76
angle of emergence 91
angle of incidence 79, 82, 87, 90
angle of reflection 79, 82, 87
angle of refraction 91
asteroids 160, 166–7
atomic number 60
atoms 58–60, 109
average speed 2

background radiation 61, 68, 165
balanced forces 13, 16
batteries *see* cells
beta radiation 62, 63, 68–9
Big Bang theory 165
biomass 38
braking distance 10
brown coal 40

cameras 99
cathode ray oscilloscopes 81–2
cells 113, 117
centre of gravity 30–1
centre of mass 30–1
centripetal force 26
charge 116, 118
   current and 113, 115
   static electricity 108–10
circuit diagrams 114
circuits
   parallel 120, 126
   potential difference in 117–18, 119, 120
   series 119–20, 125
circular motion 25–6
comets 160, 167
compressions 74, 76
Controlled Assessment Task 177–8
converging lenses 94, 95, 96–8, 100
crumple zones 19–20
crust 170
current 113–14
   alternating 133
   charge and 113, 115
   direct 133
   induced 149–51
   magnetic fields and 143–4, 145–8
   measuring 114
current–voltage graphs 124

data
   reliability of 47
   validity of 47
d.c. electric motor 147–8
deceleration 4, 14
density
   of the Earth 170
   of materials 22–4
diffuse reflection 88
diodes 121, 124
direct current 133
dispersion 92
displacement 1, 6, 7
distance 1
distance–time graphs 5–6
diverging lenses 94, 95–6
domestic appliances 49
Doppler effect 163–4
double insulation 136
drag 9, 10

Earth, structure of 84, 170–4
earthquakes 170, 172
earth wires 111, 136
echoes 82
efficiency 47–9
electrical energy 116, 118, 130
electrical power 131–2
electric current *see* current
electricity 108
   generation 39, 152
   in the home 133–7
   paying for 136–7
   safety 134–6
   transmission 112, 152–3
   units 125
electric motors 46–7, 147–8
electromagnetic induction 149–51
electromagnetic spectrum 101
electromagnetic waves 101–4
electromagnets 144–5
electromotive force 117
electrons 58, 59, 109, 113
electrostatic force 26, 109, 110
endoscopes 94
energy
   efficiency 47–9
   electrical 116, 118, 130
   forms 36
   gravitational potential 36, 37, 49–51
   kinetic 36, 37, 52–3
   law of conservation of 36
   resources 36, 37–40, 41
   in waves 74
   work and 42–4
energy flow diagrams 36–7
equilibrium 32

filament bulbs 124
Fleming's left-hand rule 146–7
focal length 95, 100
forces
   centripetal 26
   electromotive 117
   electrostatic 26, 109, 110
   frictional 9–10, 26, 48
   magnetic 144, 145–8
   moments of 26–9
   momentum and 18–19
   in a straight line 13–16
fossil fuels 38, 39, 41, 110
frequency 75
friction 9–10, 26, 48, 109
fuses 135

gamma radiation 62, 63, 69, 101, 102
gases, density of 24
Geiger-Müller tube 67–8
geostationary satellites 163
geothermal energy 38, 41
graphs
   current–voltage 124
   distance–time 5–6
   velocity–time 6–7
gravitational field strength 21, 49–50
gravitational potential energy 36, 37, 49–51
grid 152–3

half-life 65–7
heat, resistance and 121
hydroelectric power 37, 41

images
   converging lenses 96–8
   diverging lenses 96
   plane mirrors 88–9
   virtual 89, 96, 98
inertia 20
infrared radiation 101, 103
infrasound 83
ionising radiation 61, 102
isotopes 60

kinetic energy 36, 37, 52–3
kinetic theory 24

law of conservation of energy 36
law of reflection 87
lenses 94–100
   converging 94, 95, 96–8, 100
   diverging 94, 95–6
light
   dispersion 92
   Doppler effect 164
   reflection 87–9, 91–2

refraction 90–2
total internal reflection 93–4
visible 101, 103, 164
see also lenses
light-dependent resistors 121
lightning 108, 111
light years 169
liquids, density of 24
lithosphere 170
longitudinal waves 74, 76
loudness 82
low polar orbit satellites 163

magnetic fields
current and 143–4, 145–8, 149–51
Earth's 170, 173–4
motor effect 145–8
magnets 143, 145
mantle 170
mass 20, 21
acceleration and 14–16, 20
centre of 30–1
mass number 60
medians 31
microwaves 101, 103, 104
mobile phones 104
moments of forces 26–9
momentum 18–19
motor effect 145–8

National Grid 152, 153
neutral equilibrium 32
Newton's first law 14
Newton's second law 15, 18, 20
non-renewable resources 38
nuclear equations 64–5
nuclear fission 69–70
nuclear fusion 41, 70–1, 167
nuclear power stations 38, 39, 69, 70
nucleus 59, 60

Ohm's law 122–3
optical fibres 93–4
ozone layer 102

paint spraying 111
parallel circuits 120, 126
photoconductors 110–11
photocopiers 110–11
photosynthesis 41, 103
pitch 81
plane mirrors 87, 88–9
planets 160, 166, 168
plane waves 78
plate tectonics 171–4
poles 143
potential difference 116–18, 119, 120

power
electrical 131–2
mechanical 44–7
principal focus 95
principle of moments 27–8
projectors 99
protons 59, 60

radar waves 101, 103
radioactivity 61
practical work 67–9
types 61–2
units 66
uses 63–4
radio waves 101, 104
rarefactions 74, 76
ray diagrams 96–8
red-shift 164
reflection
diffuse 88
light 87–9, 91–2
sound waves 82
total internal reflection 93–4
water waves 79, 91–2
refraction
light 90–2
sound waves 92
water waves 79–80, 91–2
reliability of data 47
renewable resources 37–8
resistance 120–3
factors affecting 128–30
measuring 122
parallel circuits 126
series circuits 125
resistors 121
retardation see deceleration
rheostats 121

satellites 162–3
scalar quantities 1
series circuits 119–20, 125
smoke precipitators 110
solar cells 37, 40
Solar System 160–3
solenoids 144–5
solids, density of 23, 24
sound waves 80–2
Doppler effect 163–4
reflection 82
refraction 92
ultrasound 80, 83–5
space travel 168–9
spectrum 92, 164
speed 1–3, 6, 26
stable equilibrium 32
stars 166, 169
static electricity 108–10

dangers 111–12
effects 112
uses 110–11
Steady State theory 165–6
substations 152
Sun 41, 70–1, 102, 164, 167

thermionic emission 58
thinking distance 10
three-pin plugs 134–5
tidal barrages 37, 39
total internal reflection 93–4
transformers 154–5
transverse waves 74–5
two-way switches 134

ultrasound 80, 83–5
ultraviolet radiation 101, 102–3
unbalanced forces 13–15, 16
Universe
future of 168
origins of 165
unstable equilibrium 32

validity of data 47
variable resistors 121
vector quantities 1
velocity 2–3, 7, 26
velocity–time graphs 6–7
vibrations 74
virtual images 89, 96, 98
visible light 101, 103, 164
volcanoes 172–3
voltage 116, 118

water waves 75, 78–80
reflection 79, 91–2
refraction 79–80, 91–2
wave equation 76–7
wavelength 75, 76
waves
behaviour 78–80
electromagnetic 101–4
energy in 74
light see light
longitudinal 74, 76
properties 75–7
reflection see reflection
refraction see refraction
as renewable resource 38, 39, 41
sound 80–5, 163–4
transverse 74–5
water 75, 78–80, 91–2
weight 21
wind farms 38, 39, 41
work 41–2
energy and 42–4

X-rays 101, 102